insight text guide

Sue Tweg & Kim Edwards

Frankenstein

Mary Shelley

First published in 2009. Reprinted in 2012, 2015, 2016, 2017, 2019, 2020, 2021, 2022, 2025, 2026.

Insight Publications Pty Ltd
3/350 Charman Road
Cheltenham VIC 3192
Australia
Tel: +61 3 8571 4950
Email: books@insightpublications.com.au

www.insightpublications.com.au

National Library of Australia Cataloguing-in-Publication entry:

Tweg, Sue.
Mary Shelley's Frankenstein : insight text guide / Sue Tweg, Kim Edwards.
1st ed.
ISBN 9781921411397 (pbk.)
Insight text guide.
Bibliography.
For secondary school age.
Shelley, Mary Wollstonecraft, 1797–1851. Frankenstein.
Edwards, Kim (Kimberley)
823.7

Other ISBNs:
9781925316360 (digital)

Cover design by The Modern Art Production Group

Proudly printed in Australia by Ligare Book Printers

contents

CHARACTER MAP

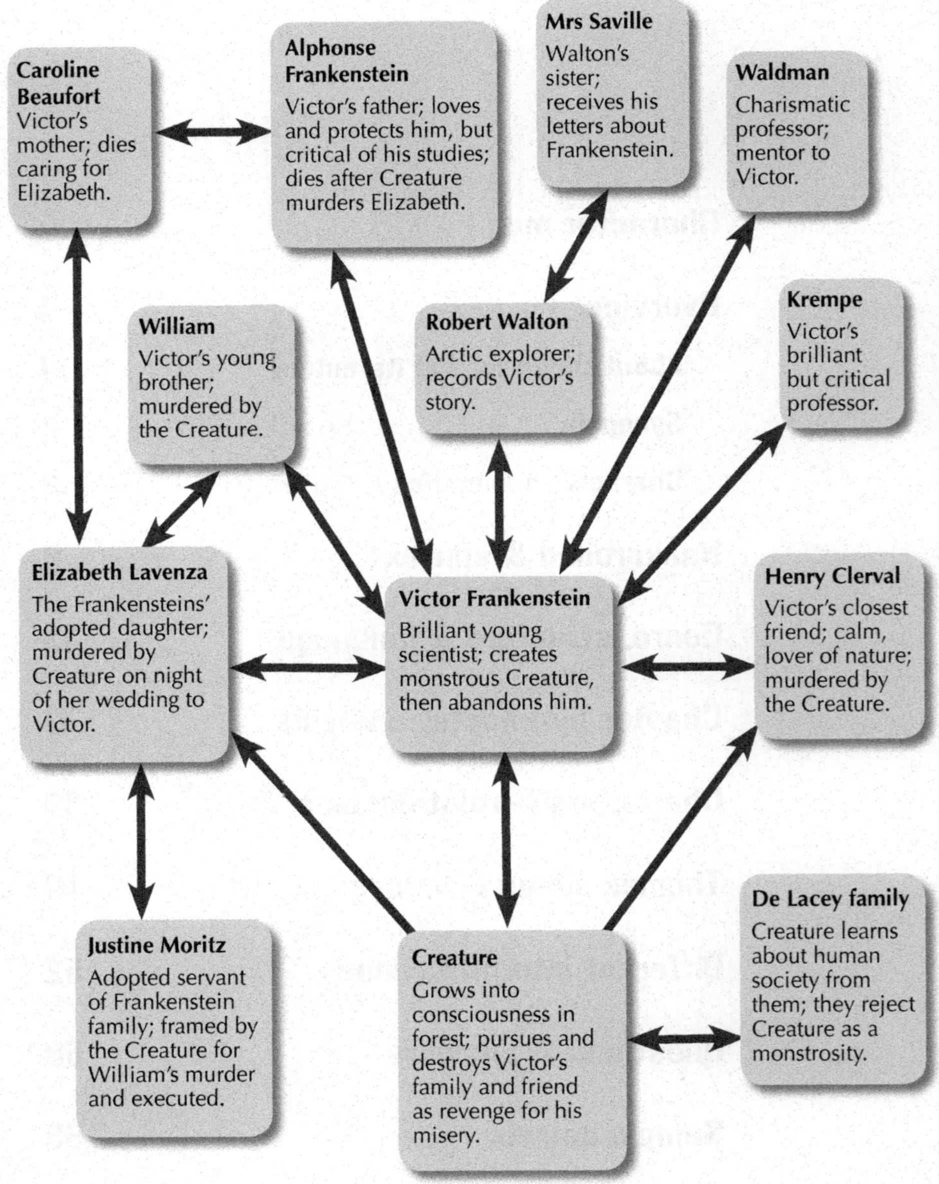

OVERVIEW

About the novel and its author

Frankenstein was published anonymously in London in 1818. It attracted immediate interest because it was generally assumed to be the work of the latest young rebel poet in town, Percy Bysshe Shelley, who certainly signed his name to the book's Preface. In fact, it was written by his 19-year-old wife, Mary. She was the daughter of famous literary parents, William Godwin and Mary Wollstonecraft (who had died giving birth to her). She had eloped with Percy to Europe four years earlier. Pregnant at 16, by the time she wrote *Frankenstein* Mary had already given birth to (and buried) two baby daughters. Her son William was to die of fever in her arms a year later. Realities of life and death circled constantly around the young couple.

Frankenstein is a horrific story of how one brilliant man, after discovering the secret of life, builds and animates a hideous Creature which he then rejects in disgust. As a consequence, the Creature goes on a rampage against the man's family and friends. Maker and Creature finally pursue each other to the death in the Arctic wasteland. The novel was a runaway success: 'It seems to be universally known and read' a friend wrote to Percy in August 1818 (Florescu, p.155).

Since then, *Frankenstein* has never been out of print, and the name 'Frankenstein' has become widely recognised, even by people who haven't read the novel, although it is often found attached mistakenly to the Creature rather than to Victor Frankenstein, the supposed creator-hero. As such, it has become a frequently heard metaphor in public speeches and media comment to indicate a once possibly good idea that has grown out of control. Not one of the many play or movie versions of the story to date has represented the material as Mary Shelley actually put it together. Remember this as you study a range of material: consider why changes might have been made.

Mary Shelley's novel interested people from the start because it went beyond a horror story to pick up serious issues of the day and present them in a highly stimulating format. She referred to her protagonist as a 'natural philosopher' (the term 'scientist' wasn't used until the mid 1830s). For his time, Victor was working at the outer limits of new scientific enquiry.

Even though 21st-century science has long moved on from 19th-century experimental guesswork, Shelley's novel continues to pinpoint key elements of an ongoing discussion about the aims and applications of knowledge. Powerful, potentially dangerous ideas continue to engage the human psyche and need to be talked about. Creative fictions like *Frankenstein* make a vital space for conversation.

Synopsis

Letters and Book One

In the Arctic, Captain Walton writes letters to his sister, revealing both his loneliness and his aspirations to be a great discoverer. Some time later, he and his crew sight a gigantic man on a sledge (the Creature). Next day, his ship takes on board a mysterious stranger (Victor Frankenstein), whose own sledge has been stranded on the breaking ice. Walton feels immediate friendship for him. When Frankenstein hears of Walton's passion for knowledge, he is motivated to tell his own tragic story, now nearing its end. It is partly a confession, partly a justification; it is also a warning to Walton, who is ignorant of the dangers inherent in satisfying his curiosity for adventure.

After filling in his childhood background, Frankenstein relates his fascination with electricity and the study of alchemy and mystic philosophy. After his mother's death, he goes to university, where he is inspired by M. Waldman, an enthusiastic chemistry professor who claims that science can reveal nature's secrets. He begins his own research into discovering 'the principle of life' and, after a period of intense study, finally succeeds in animating lifeless flesh. Frankenstein goes on to build a monstrous human being, but, when he brings it to life, he is so appalled by its appearance that he rejects both his creation and science, and has a nervous breakdown.

Two years later, restored by natural scenery and Henry Clerval's friendship, Frankenstein thinks he is free to go on with life. Meanwhile, the Creature has begun to take revenge on the creator who abandoned him by murdering William and Justine, two people Frankenstein loves.

Book Two

Frankenstein is haunted by guilt and despair but cannot reveal what he knows. Eventually, a confrontation occurs with the Creature, who hides 'alone and miserable' in the icy mountains around Chamonix.

The Creature demands that Frankenstein listen to the long story of his innocent attempts (over two years) to grow up, learn about the natural world, learn to read books and discover his horrific self. He explains how undeservedly and cruelly he has been rejected by the humans he has tried to communicate with; this has made him vengeful. He concludes by extracting a reluctant promise from Frankenstein to begin the creation of a female mate for him.

Book Three

Before marrying Elizabeth as planned, Frankenstein makes an excuse to his family so that he can spend another year alone. Continually watched by the Creature, he retreats to a remote island to work on a female mate, but is so overwhelmed by guilt that he rips apart his second creation. Enraged, the Creature first kills Frankenstein's friend Clerval and then Elizabeth, on her wedding night. Because no one believes Frankenstein's horrific story of the real murderer, he becomes the lonely avenger, doomed to wander after the equally lonely Creature to the ends of the earth. This is where he meets Walton, and dies before completing his revenge.

Finally, Walton encounters the Creature on board, mourning Frankenstein, before it goes to destroy itself in the ice field. The Creature's last speech makes Walton understand better the tragically complex relationship experienced by creator and creature.

Character summaries

Captain Walton

Twenty-eight years old; Arctic explorer; ambitious but lonely. He records the story of Frankenstein's and the Creature's lives in letters to sister Margaret. Forced by natural dangers and mutinous crew to give up voyage of discovery.

Mrs Margaret Saville

Walton's elder sister. Understood to be recipient of Walton's letters – an essential link in the complex narrative chain, although she has no direct role in plot.

Victor Frankenstein

Late 20s but seems older; a brilliant but flawed man who creates a creature that becomes his enemy when he rejects it. He dies on Walton's ship after telling the tragic story of his life.

The Creature

Develops mentally from infancy to adulthood in the few years from his creation to self-destruction after Frankenstein's death. He begins as an innocent but turns into a murderous enemy of humans after being rejected. Narrates his story to Frankenstein, who incorporates it into his narrative to Walton.

Henry Clerval

Victor's contemporary and closest friend; son of 'narrow-minded trader' who prevents him from studying with Victor at Ingolstadt. Helps nurse Frankenstein to health after his collapse; murdered by the Creature. He never asks about the secret that haunts Victor, and Frankenstein deliberately fails to confide in him.

William Frankenstein

About five years old; Victor's brother; murdered by Creature as revenge against Frankenstein.

Justine

Early 20s; young woman in Frankenstein's household; accused of William's murder by evidence planted on her by the Creature. Her execution compounds Frankenstein's guilt for rejecting the Creature.

Elizabeth Lavenza

Late 20s; nobleman's daughter adopted into Frankenstein family; manages household when Victor's mother dies; anticipated wife for Victor but murdered on wedding night as revenge for Frankenstein's destruction of the Creature's mate.

Alphonse Frankenstein

Victor's gentle elderly father, public figure in Geneva; married late in life to Caroline Beaufort. He tries to help Victor find happiness in life; collapses and dies after Elizabeth's murder.

Caroline Beaufort

Victor's loving mother, dies (when Victor is 17) of highly contagious scarlet fever caught from Elizabeth.

Krempe

A 'squat little man' with 'repulsive countenance', professor of natural philosophy at Ingolstadt university; an intelligent egocentric modern thinker, whose blunt, contemptuous manner frustrates young Victor by making him feel ignorant.

Waldman

Charismatic and benevolent professor of natural philosophy (chemistry) at Ingolstadt university; charms Victor back to enthusiastic and ambitious study.

De Lacey

Parisian exile; old, blind father of Felix and Agatha; living in forest cottage near Ingolstadt. Through observation and eavesdropping, the Creature begins to absorb a complete education from this family while secretly helping them in daily tasks. Because of his blindness, he's chosen by the Creature as first contact and is sympathetic.

Felix

A sad young man, thwarted by Safie's ungrateful father from marrying her when they escaped from France to Italy. He drives the Creature away, mistaking its approach to his father as a threat.

Agatha

The gentle young sister of Felix; faints with horror on seeing the Creature.

Safie

Beautiful 'Arabian'; wife of Felix. Daughter of Christian Arab mother and Turkish 'Mahometan' (Moslem) father. Her courageous actions to be reunited with Felix teach the Creature about the power of love.

BACKGROUND & CONTEXT

Mary Shelley

Key quote

'What terrified me will terrify others ...' (*Author's Introduction* 1831, p.9)

Percy Shelley was aware that Mary's novel contained extraordinary material, guaranteed to disturb readers. Best-selling author Sir Walter Scott was one of the few positive reviewers. He thought it 'excites new reflections and untried sources of emotion' in the reader (in *Blackwood's Edinburgh Magazine*, March 1818).

The third edition (1831) was revised and prefaced by Mary Shelley herself. By then, she was a widow (Percy had drowned in a boating accident in 1822), a woman writer claiming ownership of her own work. *Frankenstein*'s fame had been established by the 1820s through many stage adaptations in London, Europe and America, with top actors playing the Creature, habitually called 'Monster'. Mary was amused by the way an 1823 playbill [flyer] noted the cast list, with ' ----, by Mr T. Cooke', commenting that 'this nameless mode of naming the unnameable is rather good' (letter, cited in Florescu, p.165).

Mary describes her 1816 nightmare and the circumstances that stimulated it as the source of *Frankenstein* (*Author's Introduction* 1831, pp.6–10). Just as classical authors often began a fictional narrative with a 'dream vision' to add plausibility to their account (by putting themselves into the fiction they could claim to be describing events, rather than fabricating them), she makes serious claims for her creative nightmare as an authentic vision. The purpose of the book is moral, to 'speak to the mysterious fears of our nature' as well as being sensational entertainment to 'awaken thrilling horror'.

In 1831 she refers to the novel as 'my hideous progeny' (child). However *Frankenstein* was inspired in 1816, Mary Shelley was well aware of the sorrowful closeness of birth and death by 1815, when her first baby died. She wrote: 'Dream that my little baby came to life again – that it had only been cold & that we rubbed it before the fire, & it lived – I awake and find no baby – I think about the little thing all day' (*Mary Shelley's Journal*, cited in Florescu, p.132).

Mary Shelley's parents

William Godwin (1756–1836) and Mary Wollstonecraft (1759–97) had a circle of friends who were leading writers, artists and natural philosophers. Their activities enrich the fabric of ideas in *Frankenstein* (which Mary dedicated to her father), so a basic grasp of them and the revolutionary times in which they were living will help you to read the text with greater understanding.

William Godwin was a radical philosopher and novelist, who published *An Enquiry Concerning Political Justice and its Influence on General Virtue and Happiness* (known as *Political Justice*) in 1793. He argued that education should be a matter of free enquiry – if people simply understood their social duties a great and peaceful society would naturally evolve, without need for laws, leaders or institutions.

Mary Wollstonecraft is best known for her *Vindication of the Rights of Woman* (1792). She was also a translator and (briefly) a governess who wrote a grim little story book of moral lessons for children called *Original Stories from Real Life* (1788), illustrated by William Blake. The exotic character of Safie in *Frankenstein*, whose courageous actions liberate her from parental tyranny and social repression, has similarities with Wollstonecraft.

Key point

In *Vindication* (Penguin, 1975, p.268), Wollstonecraft made a very telling psychological observation about 'monsters' that could be applied interestingly to Frankenstein: 'A great proportion of the misery that wanders in hideous forms around the world is allowed to rise from the negligence of parents'.

She never had much chance to be Mary's parent because she died of childbirth complications. As a consequence, *Frankenstein* has been scrutinised for unconscious expressions of daughter Mary's guilt for causing her mother's death and for signs of ambivalence about childbearing and parenting. Victor Frankenstein is doubly culpable, first for his unnatural act of reanimating dead flesh to 'give birth', then as the neglectful mother/father of his monstrous Creature. See 'Different Interpretations' for more discussion of this idea.

Revolutionary times

The great revolutions of the late 18th century in America (1775) and France (1789) influenced Mary Shelley's world profoundly. Idealists saw the beginning of a worldwide new society, while rationalists urged caution and conservative thinkers predicted the end of civilised life. Notice how all these viewpoints surface in *Frankenstein*.

Revolutionary thinking

Walton is led to exploration, Frankenstein to natural philosophy, and the Creature to social self-education by the books they read. Find out as much as you can about writers, artists and thinkers whose work shaped people's ideas and imagination at this time. The short list below is of special relevance to *Frankenstein* and the Romantic Gothic genre.

Plutarch (c. AD 46–120). Greek historian of the Roman world. His influential book, *Lives of the Greeks and Romans*, was widely read in translation, and a source for Shakespeare's Roman plays. Plutarch saw history in terms of biographies of famous leaders, their strengths and weaknesses and general moral qualities.

John Milton (1608–74). English poet, revolutionary political thinker and writer. Milton wrote his epic poem *Paradise Lost* to 'justify the ways of God to men', explaining the divine purpose of allowing proud Lucifer's first rebellion and fall from heaven into Pandemonium (Hell). He loses his 'bright' name and becomes Satan 'the adversary'; he then causes Adam and Eve's fall and expulsion from the Garden of Eden. *Paradise Lost* raises complex and subtle questions about good and evil, free will, heroism and suffering. Lucifer/Satan is characterised so strongly and sympathetically that William Blake later claimed Milton had been 'a true Poet and of the Devil's party without knowing it' (that is, not bound by religious conventions). Milton continues to be admired for using rational argument to challenge bigotry about ethical issues like censorship and divorce.

Key passage

Frankenstein's Creature reads *Paradise Lost* and is deeply affected by it, drawing parallels between himself, Lucifer and Adam, as all cast away by their creator (pp.132–4). He says to Frankenstein, 'I ought to be thy Adam, but I am rather the fallen angel' (p.103). Later, Victor identifies himself with 'the archangel who aspired to omnipotence' (p.214).

William Blake (1757–1827). English visionary poet, artist and freethinker. Blake thought that free imagination was the essential 'God' quality in humans. His above comment on Milton comes from *The Marriage of Heaven and Hell* (1790), which proposes to unite human impulses of creative freedom and rational restraint into a new synthesis of revolutionary 'progression'. His two books of poetry, *Songs of Innocence* (1789) and *Songs of Experience* (1794), explore how the Romantic poet views the inevitable corruption of childlike perceptions with experience of socialisation, especially through fear-inducing religion and mind-numbing routine.

Samuel Taylor Coleridge (1772–1834). Romantic poet, philosopher, friend of Godwin. His *Rime of the Ancient Mariner* is quoted in *Frankenstein*.

Johann Wolfgang von Goethe (1749–1832). Influential German Romantic writer, botanist, philosopher. Two of his works are relevant to *Frankenstein*: *The Sorrows of Young Werther* (1774), and *Faust* (Part One, 1808). The Creature reads the story of noble, doomed Werther (Volume Two, Chapter VII) who lived, loved, suffered and killed himself honourably. Victor is linked with the brilliant scientist who trades his soul to the Devil in return for forbidden knowledge. Frankenstein finds his devil in M. Waldman, who seduces him with scientific knowledge, then torments him with praise for what he's accomplished (p.69), leading to others suffering for his 'unhallowed arts' (p.90). In the end, love saves Goethe's Faust – but not Frankenstein. Like Christopher Marlowe's Faustus (from his 1592 play, *Dr Faustus*), Frankenstein loses hope and succumbs to despair.

Jean-Jacques Rousseau (1712–78). Influential French philosopher, writer. Mary Godwin would have encountered Rousseau's works in her father's library. *Discourse on the Origins and Foundations of Inequality Amongst Men* (1754) argued that there was no original sin; humans were born good and made bad by institutions. *The Social Contract* (1762) argued – among much else – that the general will of the people should rule. *The Confessions* (1781) is an autobiographical account of how a 'man of feeling' experiences life. Every event leaves its mark. This work's key ideas – on the innocence of childhood and of primitive society – have many echoes in *Frankenstein*, especially in the Creature's journey of self-discovery. His opening lines may have influenced Frankenstein's narrative: 'I was born in Geneva in 1712 ...'

John Locke (1632–1704). *An Essay Concerning Human Understanding* (1690) has some similarities with Rousseau in relation to how humans acquire understanding through experience and reflection; another influential work that Mary Shelley knew and used to structure her Creature's developing awareness of himself and others.

Count Volney Constantin (1757–1820). His *Ruins; or a Survey of the Revolutions of Empire* (1791), known as *Ruins of Empires*, promoted atheistic humanism. It was an influential work for the Shelleys and the book from which the Creature learns idealistic revolutionary concepts (p.122).

Edmund Burke (1729–97). *Philosophical Enquiry into the Origin of our Ideas of the Sublime and Beautiful* (1756) was a key text for writers trying to work out just why the scenery of the natural world had such a powerful effect on humans. He's important for Gothic Romantic writers because he links natural beauty with terror – when we are astonished (his word) by nature's vastness and power we feel both excited and strained (in nerves and muscles). Reading poetry about it and seeing paintings of wild nature, or listening to the emotionally charged music of Beethoven, has the same stimulating effect.

Frankenstein's science

Key quotes

'Natural philosophy is the genius that has regulated my fate ...' (p.40)

'None but those who have experienced them can conceive of the enticements of science.' (p.51)

The century-and-a-half leading up to the publication of *Frankenstein*, beginning with the foundation of the Royal Society in 1660, had also witnessed revolutionary change in the sciences. To get a taste of the times, you can look up famous discoveries and inventions of **William Harvey, Isaac Newton, Erasmus Darwin, Humphrey Davy, George Stephenson, Luigi Galvani**, **Count Alessandro Volta** and **Michael Faraday** (to select a few of the many great inventor-discoverers in England, Europe and America).

Thinking people didn't have to identify themselves with either arts or sciences at this time: their curiosity ranged everywhere. Isaac Newton, for example, was a famous theoretical mathematician, an experimental alchemist, a leading public servant (Master of the Royal Mint) and a mystic – and he designed the first practical domestic cat-flap for his pet at home. *The Lunar Men* by Jenny Uglow is an excellent account of the flood of 18th-century discoveries and inventions, especially relating to electricity, which is the animating principle, 'a spark of being' (p.58), in *Frankenstein*. Galvani's electrical experiments with frogs' legs in the 1780s (demonstrating electrical impulses to stimulate muscle contractions) fascinated Percy Shelley.

Mary and Percy attended several popular lecture demonstrations in London, including one on 'Electricity and the Elements' by Andrew Crosse in December 1814. Crosse, a fascinating enthusiast who may have partly inspired Mary's depiction of Victor Frankenstein, spent much of his life working out how to harness electricity drawn from thunderstorms. Locals thought his work diabolical. He may also be the basis for Colin Clive's 'mad scientist' Frankenstein in the 1931 film version (his story is told in *The Man who was Frankenstein* by Peter Haining).

Victor Frankenstein is attracted to the work of early experimenters like:

- **Albertus Magnus** (1193–1280). Dominican monk, theologian, botanist, magician; he looked at brain function and speech (and was supposedly the creator of a 'brazen head' speaking automaton).
- **Cornelius Agrippa** (1486–1535). Physician, astrologer and magician.
- **Paracelsus** (1493–1541). Physician and alchemist, he claimed to have discovered how to make 'homunculus' or 'little man'.

Even though they did not perform modern experimental science (no one would until centuries later), early mystical alchemists attempted to acquire knowledge of the natural world, as they understood it to be made, so that it could be integrated with the dominant Western Christian world view. Alchemy is still popularly thought of as the work of power-hungry individuals hoping to get rich (by finding the Philosopher's Stone and creating gold) or achieve immortality (by discovering the Elixir of Life). More realistically it can be thought of as proto-science, where serious experimenters developed new understandings of substances and chemical processes as they searched for even greater secrets of nature.

Frankenstein's father and his professors dismiss the alchemists, but modern natural philosophy bores Frankenstein; it lacks the glamour of old mysticism. He laments that at least 'such views, although futile, were grand ...' (p.48). Professor Waldman rekindles Frankenstein's ambition by linking mystical ambition to the new science with its 'unlimited powers' (p.49).

Q Would you call Frankenstein's idea of discovering the mechanisms of life itself in order to gain power over natural processes 'science'?

Sir Humphrey Davy (1778–1829) was a philosopher, chemist, electrician, inventor, boy wonder, poet, and professor of chemistry at the newly founded Royal Institution. He was also a friend of Coleridge and Godwin. Research his life and work for an idea of how a brilliant man, very similar to Victor Frankenstein, developed his passionate enthusiasm for natural science.

Promethean work

Mythic references to **Prometheus** identify him as a creative rebel, challenging the supreme authority of the Greek gods, who wanted exclusive use of their powerful knowledge. He stole fire, gave it to humans and taught them all the useful arts. In the Roman version, he stole creative material itself, shaped it with earth and gave life to humans. As punishment, Zeus had him bound to a rock, where he endured perpetual torture: his liver was devoured by a vulture each day, only to grow again each night. The novel's full title *Frankenstein; or, The Modern Prometheus* indicates that it is about 'big' questions (see 'Themes, Ideas and Values'). The Promethean impulse in humans is about intelligence and how to use it, but it also suggests the transgression of rules, with the terrible punishment that might result. Walton, Frankenstein and the Creature are a trio of Prometheans on risky quests.

When Shelley refers to 'the mysterious fears of our nature' in her 1831 introduction, she reminds us of the ambiguous relationship humans have with knowledge. The word 'mystery' itself implies that there are things beyond rational knowledge and empirical testing. Fear is inevitably associated with not knowing. The genre of the horror story itself attracts readers by offering an imaginative peek into the unknown. In contrast, science, by its very name, is about knowing; it is about the knowledge gained through facts, rather than fancy. Frankenstein's search to know the secrets of nature is really about discovering 'the final cause'; that is, where life itself originates.

In Mary Shelley's time it was becoming more common to express atheistic views and look for explanations to life's mysteries in the material world itself, rather than in supernatural causes. Many natural philosophers, like Erasmus Darwin, Joseph Priestley and Humphrey

Davy, saw no conflict between spirituality and rational enquiry, while people with a more traditional religious faith still thought of life as only properly knowable to a creator god. This is another basic issue debated in *Frankenstein*.

GENRE, STRUCTURE & LANGUAGE

Genre

The Gothic horror story

This genre has been popular in England since the mid 1700s. Shelley claims that she wants to 'awaken thrilling horror' (*Author's Introduction* 1831, p.8) and a reviewer of the second edition (1823) described it as 'the best instance of natural passion applied to supernatural events' (cited in Florescu, p.156). Key features of the Gothic horror genre relevant to *Frankenstein* are: an experience of terror beyond fears or anxieties; and a general sense of insecurity in characters, who face potential physical violence, psychological threats and repeated nervous collapse. Encounters are set in gloomy interiors of ancient places, in darkness (or possibly moonlight), with hostile natural conditions. Nature is a sublime crushing force. Death and physical decay are emphasised. Gothic narratives abound with uncanny characters like doubles (*doppelgängers*), ghosts and vampires, the damned souls of brave overreachers (like Dr Faustus) or doomed undying wanderers (like the Wandering Jew, the Flying Dutchman, or the Ancient Mariner) who are able to cross the normally observed boundaries between the living and the dead. Living humans may turn out to be maniacs, psychopaths (it's possible to interpret Frankenstein this way), hysterics, or otherwise unstable or deranged obsessives. There is a useful discussion of generic terms and the social purpose of horror in King (1982), Punter (1996, Chapter 4), Mulvey-Roberts (1998) and Davenport-Hines (1998).

Gothic romance

The word 'Romance' as used in a Gothic sense comes from *roman*, an adventure story set in historical times, with wandering knights – young Henry Clerval dreams his life will turn out to be like one of them (p.39). Romance also includes fantasy and the supernatural, often building adventures around a quest motif or an epic journey. Percy Shelley wrote that a supernatural tale 'affords a point of view to the imagination for the delineating of human passions more comprehensive and commanding than any which the ordinary relations of existing events can yield' (1818 *Preface*, p.11). *Frankenstein* deals with human passions in 'commanding' (melodramatic, sensational) detail.

Science fiction

How much real 'science' content is required in this genre? The answer is often surprisingly little. Think of films you know. The story may be nominally set in the future but is less concerned with scientific predictions than with adventure, often with a quest motif (Will the brilliant scientist make the vaccine in time? Will the hero manage to destroy the alien threat?). Usually included is an underlying critique of worrying contemporary scientific trends. Science fiction foregrounds strong moral and ethical ideas: think about H. G. Wells, Ursula le Guin, *Blade Runner, Gattaca, Independence Day*. Brian Aldiss' *Frankenstein Unbound* (1973) is an interesting spin-off science fiction story using Shelley's narrative techniques.

Novel of ideas

Although Shelley wanted readers to be entertained by her story, it was not meant to be simply an action-packed, quick read with thrillingly melodramatic incident after incident (which is what it tended to become on stage and in film versions). See 'Themes, Ideas and Values' for details about the many 'big' ideas in *Frankenstein*.

Structure

The novel can be difficult to read at first because its structure is complex. Like the Creature itself, the structure has been created from disparate parts, brought together to make a whole. It is an epistolary novel (made up of a series of letters). Walton narrates the tale to his sister through the letters (which we also read), Frankenstein narrates to Walton, and the Creature narrates to Frankenstein (and then briefly to Walton at the end). This gives the story a sense of immediacy and credibility because it is comprised of 'eyewitness' accounts and invites us to consider how the tale is told, by whom, to whom, and how it is being passed on.

Frankenstein uses a *layered* technique, where one set of ideas is imposed upon another and then upon another. Walton, Frankenstein and the Creature are constantly processing what happens to them. The Creature especially reflects on developing awareness of bodily sensation and feelings. Self-educated (according to Rousseau's and Godwin's principles), he constructs his own sensitive, morally aware personhood: the reader comes to understand how his cruel imprisonment in a monstrous body leads to negative personality changes.

The Creature's embedded narrative

This is literally the heart of the story. Only the Creature knows what happened after Frankenstein abandoned him, leaving him to discover the world alone, like a newborn child. Miraculously, he survived, educated himself and turned bitter towards humanity through ill-treatment. His diabolical nature, which is all we've heard about from Frankenstein, somehow doesn't square with the Creature's own highly articulate account of things, as he tells it to Frankenstein, who then makes it part of the ongoing story he is telling to Walton. Notice that within the Creature's narrative there are two further stories – the history of the De Laceys and Safie's story.

The Creature seems forever caged by Frankenstein's story, whether he likes it or not. Or is he? Frankenstein apparently reports the Creature's narrative truthfully, word for word. Do our ideas of Frankenstein change as we hear the Creature's view of things? How does Frankenstein respond? Does he consider his responsibility for the Creature in a new light at all?

Frankenstein's main narrative

Victor tells Walton how he grew up, created the Creature, rejected it, met it again (this is where the Creature's *embedded* narrative is located), and how the Creature and he are fated to pursue each other. Frankenstein's narrative is influential because it seems to tell the whole story to us, recounted accurately, word for word, by Walton to his sister. Through Walton's uncritical hero-worship of his newly found friend, we are initially inclined to give this narrative credence and feel empathy with the suffering protagonist. However, as the story unfolds and we get our own sense of Victor's character, Shelley invites us to read against the grain and reconsider Frankenstein as the hero–protagonist. Is he a completely reliable narrator, especially when it comes to explaining his motives?

Walton's framing narrative

A good picture frame matches and sets off the picture it surrounds, without drawing our attention from the main object of interest, the picture within it. Similarly, Walton's narrative begins on a boastful note but also suggests a life of bleakness – he's a lonely man in a very dangerous environment. Walton tells his sister that he expects to be either famous or lost: either way, he'll be immortalised by his letters. His situation prepares the reader for Frankenstein's more devastating account of aspiration and danger already endured.

Finally, notice that the narrative is in a ring structure. Thus we have the outer, encircling story of Walton (framing narrative), the inner enclosed story of Frankenstein (main narrative), and the central story of the Creature (embedded narrative). Traditionally, a ring structure is emblematic of an epic, heroic quest narrative. The hero sets out from his place of origin, has a series of adventures, overcomes obstacles and fights monsters. He descends into hell (literally or figuratively) in the middle of the story, faces similar trials on the way home, and finally returns to where he began, understanding the world and himself better than before. How is this text both using and challenging this structural formula? Is there a hero? Is there an heroic quest?

Language

Shelley's use of language is formal. Her sentence structures and vocabulary constantly link *Frankenstein* to the powerful literary and philosophical language of her sources for ideas, especially Milton, Rousseau, Goethe and the Romantic poets who were all great talkers and writers. Notice how language patterns vary, giving different textures to the narrative and helping to reveal character.

Read Elizabeth's letter to Victor (Book One, Chapter VI). Notice how the epistolary style gives the writer freedom to suggest informality through greetings and endearments, and to articulate delicate thoughts sincerely. Letters in themselves remind us how precarious this narrative is, and also how private, how personal. Are Walton's letters really meant for the eyes of the world to read? What do their construction and tone tell us about Walton's relationship with his far-distant sister?

Sometimes the language is in the form of a conversation, sometimes of a monologue or a quarrel. Even here, something odd happens through the language we read, if we pay attention to who's speaking. A passionate conversation, apparently recalled word for word with every emotion represented, is actually a reported event. Look at when Victor and the Creature argue near Chamonix. In fact, Victor is telling Walton about this scene, long after it occurred, although the emotions of both the Creature and Victor are vividly articulated.

Walton, Frankenstein and the Creature are linked by their parallel narratives, their similarities as men on quests. How does each one's characteristic language distinguish them? The Creature finds its 'knowledge quest' when it perceives the intrinsic power of language as a system to make communication possible ('This was indeed a godlike science, and I ardently desired to become acquainted with it' – p.115). This remains his prime aim until the end of his last conversation with Walton at the end of the book.

CHAPTER-BY-CHAPTER ANALYSIS

Author's Introduction 1831

Mary Shelley's introduction to the third edition reinforces its, and her own, 'Gothic' literary credentials. With Shelley and Byron both dead, she elaborates on the process of Frankenstein's creation out of her aspiration to prove her younger self as a writer 'worthy of [her] parentage' (p.6) and competent to mix with great Romantic poets. She relates her own literary task to contemporary scientific work (the apparent miracle of animation Erasmus Darwin accomplished in his laboratory with wriggling vermicelli, and Galvani's experiments with the mysterious force of electricity demonstrated on frogs' legs).

While being aware of its blasphemous potential (p.9), Shelley wants to support the science of her novel as at least partially based in the facts as they were then understood. She is also keen to assert the deep veracity of her dream, which feels more like a revelation than a nightmare.

Q If the disturbing dream is a prophetic warning, what is its message? For whom? About what? Maybe Frankenstein communicates the message.

Original Preface 1818

Percy Shelley writes in first-person authorial voice, speaking for Mary: s/he cites the prestigious name of Dr Darwin on the second line to alert readers to the kind of subject matter they are likely to find. Notice the tone of wistfulness at being left alone with her 'ghostly visions' (while Shelley and Byron walk in the Alps); it combines with another tone of quiet triumph (as the most inexperienced writer among the literary group) to be the only one to complete a publishable 'tale' (p.12).

Volume One

Letter I

The novel begins with the framing narrative of Captain Robert Walton writing sometime in the late 1700s from St Petersburg in Northern Russia to his sister Margaret Saville in London. He looks forward to his journey of exploration to the North Pole as a glorious adventure, for '[w]hat may not be expected in a country of eternal light?' (p.15). He ends the letter with a heartfelt farewell, for if he should fail in his goal, 'you will see me again soon, or never' (p.18).

Q What are Walton's anticipations for his adventure in this opening letter? What tone is being set for the narrative to follow?

Letter II

Three months later, Walton has made it as far north as Archangel (notice the significance of the place name for someone embarked on an epic quest) – but confesses he is lonely. He explains how important and affirming friendship can be, and laments that good employees cannot make up for lack of a friend. He is resolute in setting out but promises to 'do nothing rashly' (p.21) because the safety of his crew is his responsibility. He also vows to 'kill no albatross' (p.21), unlike the unfortunate sailor in Coleridge's poem *The Rime of the Ancient Mariner*.

Q What does Walton desire from a friend? How does his idealised view of friendship inform other kinds of relationships in the novel?

Letter III

Another three months have passed. Walton has safely begun his sea voyage and promises to be 'cool, persevering and prudent' (p.23). He's also determined to succeed in his quest and proceed over 'the untamed yet obedient element' of icy sea (p.24).

Q Walton asks: 'What can stop the determined heart and resolved will of man?' (p.24). Can you think of any answers?

Letter IV

A month later, this letter not only marks the crew's (and our) first glimpse of 'a being … the shape of a man, but apparently of gigantic stature' (p.25); it features the important meeting of Walton and Victor Frankenstein. Walton is fascinated with his unexpected guest, found alone and near death in the icy wasteland. He had longed for a friend, and the extraordinary opportunity leads to hero worship in Walton for the eloquent mystery man with his wild mood swings and relentless determination.

As they continue north and Frankenstein's health improves, Walton explains he would sacrifice everything to succeed in his enterprise. The visitor calls such aspiration 'madness', and tells his story as a warning: 'Have you drunk also of the intoxicating draught? Hear me – let me reveal my tale, and you will dash the cup from your lips!' (p.29).

This section is full of florid descriptions, passionate language, and close attention to feelings and senses, emphasising Walton's idolisation and Frankenstein's frenzied state of mind. It also anticipates how the story will deal with immense concepts about the future of science, the mysteries of nature, and the fate of humanity.

Q What specific hints are being offered in this chapter regarding what is to come?

Chapter I

Walton's framing narrative ends and Frankenstein's main narrative begins. He tells his family history. It includes the rescue of his angelic child-mother by his kindly benevolent father, their devoted care of him, and the procurement of Elizabeth Lavenza as an adopted daughter and Victor's 'gift'. Stress is laid on the importance of good parenting and familial love. Victor's mother and father are very conscious of the responsibility of bringing up an 'innocent and helpless' child (p.35). His happy childhood in Geneva contrasts significantly with the torment of the man we have just met.

Chapter II

Growing up, Frankenstein develops a 'thirst for knowledge' – he desires to 'learn the hidden laws of nature' (p.38), and his curiosity is insatiable. At school, Victor becomes close friends with Henry Clerval. While Victor is passionate to know 'the secrets of heaven and earth' (p.39), 'knightly' Henry is interested in the virtues of humanity. Clerval's morality is something his friend comes to admire and appreciate deeply.

Frankenstein tells us that '[n]atural philosophy is the genius that has regulated my fate' (p.40), but his study of physics began with outdated texts and outlandish ideas, and his schoolboy dreams were more of fame and glory than science. The destruction of an old tree near his house once kindled a passion to investigate electricity and mathematics; Victor now sees it as a metaphor: destiny's laws are more potent than science, and these childhood studies have led to his 'utter and terrible destruction' (p.43).

Q What kind of student is Frankenstein? What factors affect what he learns – and what he fails to learn?

Chapter III

When he is 17, Victor's mother dies nursing his adopted sister through scarlet fever. She expresses the wish that Victor and Elizabeth will one day marry, and passes her maternal role to Elizabeth. This first experience of sorrow and loss affects Frankenstein severely – he calls death 'that most irreparable evil' (p.45), and his grief later fuels his scientific pursuits. He leaves reluctantly for Ingolstadt university.

Key point

Saying goodbye to his family, Elizabeth and Henry, Victor leaves behind all they provide for him: love, stability, and a check to his tendency towards obsession and amorality.

At university his dislike of Professor Krempe drives Frankenstein obstinately to return to his study of ancient texts. However, his veneration of Waldman inspires him to learn innovative sciences. Frankenstein thus pursues not only the old teachers, like Agrippa and Paracelsus, who 'promised impossibilities', but the modern masters with 'new and almost unlimited powers' (p.49). He believes this powerful and intoxicating combination 'decided my future destiny' (p.50).

Q 'The labours of men of genius, however erroneously directed, scarcely ever fail in ultimately turning to the solid advantage of mankind' (p.50). Do you agree?

Chapter IV

Two years pass as Victor studies, pondering fundamental questions of life and death. He turns his attentions to gruesome and sacrilegious research. He collects body parts, watches corpses decay, and begins experimenting until he is 'capable of bestowing animation upon lifeless matter' (p.53).

Frankenstein then interrupts his own story to tell Walton (and us) that he refuses to reveal this secret, and warns his tale will have a moral: 'listen patiently until the end of my story, and you will easily perceive why I am reserved upon that subject' (p.54). He explains how utterly obsessed he was with his horrific loathsome pursuits, and how, as the seasons passed, he was oblivious to nature's beauty, neglectful of his family, and became nervous, paranoid and feverish.

Q What imagery and what kinds of language are being used here to describe the act of creation?

Chapter V

In November (a 'birth' into ice and snow), Frankenstein brings his 'creation' to life. But he is horrified at the sight of the being that was designed to be 'beautiful' (p.58) and immediately abandons his work. His sleep is then troubled with dreams of kissing a blooming Elizabeth, who turns into his mother's worm-eaten corpse. He wakes to find the hideous Creature muttering and reaching over the bed. Victor flees the house in terror.

Henry Clerval arrives unexpectedly to find Victor hysterical with unexplained joy; the Creature has disappeared, but Victor is on the verge of a nervous breakdown. Devoted and self-sacrificing, Henry gives up his education for months to nurse Victor back to health as spring comes around.

Q Why is Frankenstein so afraid of what he has created?

Chapter VI

Henry begins his hard-won education, but Frankenstein suffers from guilt and distress when his professors praise his scientific progress. The two friends begin studying eastern languages and humanities, and Victor is relieved to put science behind him. The friends take a walking tour; Henry's invigorating, affectionate company and the beautiful landscapes and warm, rejuvenating May weather restore Frankenstein's health and spirits.

Q After his long self-exile and illness, Frankenstein returns to the world. What is he rediscovering?

Chapter VII

Victor's father writes with the tragic news that William has been murdered, and begs him to return to Geneva. The journey home is an emotional one for Frankenstein, fluctuating between anguish and joy in returning to his family. He has been away for six years, and it is now two years since his fatal experiment drew breath.

Outside Secheron, Victor has a premonition of disaster and visits the site of William's murder in a 'beautiful yet terrific' thunderstorm (p.77). The environment reflects his inner tempest, until a flash of lighting (recalling the blasted oak tree) reveals a glimpse of the Creature: 'the filthy daemon to whom I had given life' (pp.77–8). Frankenstein leaps to the conclusion that he is the murderer, for '[n]othing in human shape could have destroyed that fair child' (p.78). This discovery arouses Victor's sense of moral responsibility; he is reunited with his grieving family and hears Justine falsely accused of the crime he himself caused unwittingly.

Q Who is accusing whom here? What reasons are given for presuming guilt?

Chapter VIII

Frankenstein suffers a double sense of guilt during Justine's trial: first for William's murder, then for her unjust sentencing. Justine cannot explain why a missing locket from the body was found on her, and even Elizabeth's compassionate plea on her behalf only ignites public anger against her.

Victor fears he will be thought mad if he tells his secret, so his revelation goes unspoken. Justine's forced confession shakes even Elizabeth's faith in the innocence of her 'sister' (p.88), but the burden of lying troubles Justine more than the accusations. She blesses and farewells Elizabeth, and is hanged as a murderess. Frankenstein expresses his enduring horror at these two 'first hapless victims to my unhallowed arts' (p.90), and the closing paragraphs hint obliquely at further death and destruction to come.

Q 'The tortures of the accused did not equal mine' (p.86). How justified is Frankenstein's claim?

Volume Two

Chapter I

Frankenstein 'wandered like an evil spirit' (p.93), envying Justine's escape from despair and remorse. His own sufferings are 'such as no language can describe' (p.93), and while the family deals with their grief and blasted innocence, he seeks solitude at Chamonix. He is awe-struck by the supreme beauty of the Alps and soothed by 'maternal nature' (p.98).

Q How do Elizabeth and Frankenstein deal with their respective grief and sense of guilt?

Chapter II

Key chapter

Nature is tranquiliser and tonic for Victor – personal problems take on a new perspective in the majestic and sublime natural surroundings. His climb up Montanvert functions as a metaphor for his former aspirations, particularly in contemplating the difference between man and brute; it culminates with the arrival of his Creature.

The first spoken meeting of this new Adam/Satan with his creator god opens with an ultimatum. The Creature insists that Frankenstein recognise his duty to the being he has brought into the world – or else it will kill everyone he loves. Victor responds with violence and anger, though the Creature insists, 'I was benevolent and good; misery has made me a fiend. Make me happy, and I shall again be virtuous' (p.103).

Key point

Like Frankenstein and his creation, the narrative itself wrestles with complex philosophical and ethical issues about the nature of humanity. Questions are raised about justice, compassion and the right to happiness, and about social, familial and even racial obligations between beings (p.103). The Creature argues for a right to be heard: his eloquence reaches across the multiple narrative layers and audiences. It applies to Victor, but also to Walton, then Margaret, and then ourselves as the final readers: 'Listen to my tale: when you have heard that, abandon or commiserate me, as you shall judge that I deserve. But hear me' (p.103).

Q What is the significance of the highly formal language used in this first encounter between Frankenstein and the Creature?

Chapter III

This marks a significant turning point in the novel. Once the Creature is given his own narrative voice, we must start rethinking both Frankenstein's representation of his creation and himself in the main narrative, along with Walton's representation of Frankenstein in the framing narrative.

The Creature tells of a fully remembered infancy – every sensation, instinctive need and developing emotion (including fear and loneliness). His fascination with the natural environment and his discovery of his own nature draw parallels with Adam in Eden and Rousseau's 'noble savage'. He experiences a catalogue of basic human needs, but his first encounters with humans provoke violent reactions. Hiding near a cottage, he observes a family who unconsciously show him true civilisation with their culture, learning and mutual affection. His amazement and delight in this 'brave new world' recollect Shakespeare's Caliban (*The Tempest*) and Milton's Satan – like Frankenstein, this 'monster' began with the best of intentions, and a sincere love for the world and humanity.

Q Create a timeline of the Creature's growth and learning in this chapter. What can you see occurring?

Chapter IV

The Creature experiences moral and emotional development by recognising unhappiness in the family and connecting it to his own experiences: misery is not an inherent state but has a cause, a reason. Like Prometheus, he is now eager to benefit humanity: he stops taking the family's food and secretly begins working around their property. The cottagers call him their unseen 'good spirit' (p.117), and he looks on them as caring gods. He comes to recognise language as a key feature of human civilisation: a 'godlike science' (p.115). He yearns to read words but realises he cannot even 'understand the sounds for which they stood as signs' (p.116).

The Creature becomes self-aware in recognising his own reflection. The philosopher Jacques Lacan identified this key moment in childhood development as the 'mirror-stage' marking a new level of sentience and intellectual sophistication. For the Creature, it's a discovery of aesthetic sensibility; he is revolted by his own ugliness, in contrast to the beauty of the family. He resolves to study hard in order to communicate with his idols, hoping they will love him back. As spring arrives, the aspiring Creature is happy and 'elevated by the enchanting appearance of nature' (p.118).

Q Add to the timeline now that the Creature is learning to reason and analyse. What things cannot be understood simply through observation?

Chapter V

When a new inhabitant arrives at the cottage, the Creature explains how the consequent events 'impressed me with feelings which, from what I had been, have made me what I am' (p.119). Felix's love Safie is Turkish, but the Creature comes to understand an important lesson: different races are permitted to mix if they are able to communicate. Language is the tool to unite them, and the Creature secretly learns it in two months along with Safie. This liberal education and thirst for knowledge recollect Frankenstein as well as Faust.

The Creature also learns the paradox of human nature: 'Was man, indeed, at once so powerful, so virtuous, and magnificent, yet so vicious and base?' (p.122). He begins contemplating his worth, and this leads to further social awareness, as he considers his lack of family and the question of his identity – 'What was I?' (p.124).

Q Like Victor, the Creature is learning the price of pursuing knowledge. What has he lost and gained?

Chapter VI

The Creature then relates the history of the De Lacey family, from Felix's well-intentioned championing of Safie's wrongly accused father, to his betrayal and their subsequent exile. Safie's racial and cultural difference is explored, as is her father's abhorrence of Christianity and his tyrannical demands upon his daughter. However, 'amor vincit omnia' (love conquers all), and Safie flees her country, her religion and her family to return to Felix.

Q What parallels can we draw between this embedded narrative and the histories of other characters in the novel?

Chapter VII

Key chapter

The Creature discovers the profound importance and delight of literature, and the emotional, educational and intellectual stimulation of books colours our own reading of the novel in hand. It notes, 'I found myself similar, yet at the same time strangely unlike to the being concerning whom I read, and in whose conversation I was a listener' (p.131). This is meta-narrative (narrative conscious of itself as narrative), for the Creature is suddenly articulating our own experience in dealing with this novel.

The texts the Creature acquires are Milton's *Paradise Lost,* Plutarch's *Lives* and Goethe's *Sorrows of Young Werther.* These masterpieces lead him to more questions about his sense of self, particularly in identifying with Milton's Adam and Satan. Reading Frankenstein's journal provides some answers, but '[i]ncrease of knowledge only discovered to me more clearly what a wretched outcast I was' (p.133). As autumn wanes, the Creature is conscious of his painful separation from humanity. He finally dares to speak with the blind father and asks for asylum, but the crucial interview is interrupted. Fear gives way to violence: Felix beats the Creature and drives him from the cottage. The Creature despairs at experiencing expulsion from 'Eden' through no fault or crime of his own. This is his 'paradise lost'.

Q What value is the reading and study of literature given here?

Chapter VIII

Rather than despair at ultimate rejection, the Creature fleas, feeling the rage of an 'archfiend' and a desire to kill nature and humanity as he 'declares everlasting war against the species' (p.138). In terms of the characters of *Paradise Lost,* the hopeful Adam has become a vengeful Satan. Returning, he discovers the cottagers have fled and 'broken the only link that held me to the world' (p.140). His fury manifests in fire – he burns down their home, and Prometheus the fire-bringer becomes the destroyer.

Wretched, the Creature sets out in search of Frankenstein, for 'on you only had I any claim for pity and redress' (p.141). Spring partly revives his spirits, until another violent rejection occurs when he saves a drowning girl and is shot by her guardian. Punishment for being deliberately kind and unintentionally hideous is becoming a familiar lesson. When the Creature reaches Geneva, he meets a possible friend: a child he hopes is too young to be prejudiced. However, the boy (Victor's brother William) calls him 'monster' and 'ogre' (p.144), and when the name Frankenstein is revealed, the Creature strangles him. Like Satan, his weapon is death – he gloats, 'I too can create desolation; my enemy is not invulnerable' (p.144). He uses William's locket to frame Justine for the crime. Woman thus becomes the source of man's crime.

Q How sympathetic are you towards the Creature by the end of his story?

Chapter IX

Like Adam requesting a mate from God, the Creature asks Frankenstein for a companion: for 'if I cannot inspire love, I will cause fear' (p.148). He imagines himself and his mate leading an Eden-like existence in harmony with nature and complete with each other in a new land, far from Europe.

Frankenstein initially refuses on the grounds that he cannot risk perpetuating a race of monsters from a diabolical Adam and Eve, but the Creature asserts that his terrible deeds are not the result of his inherent character: 'I am malicious because I am miserable' (p.147). Moved by his eloquence and reasoning, Frankenstein finally agrees and the Creature leaves, satisfied. Victor travels home to Geneva to begin a task that horrifies him – he must plan a female monster.

Q 'I shall … become linked to the chain of existence and events from which I am now excluded' (p.150). From what is the Creature excluded? What will its 'prayer' link it to?

Volume Three

Chapter I

Making a mate for the Creature repulses Victor; taking one for himself seems acceptable. Frankenstein's father suggests he marry Elizabeth, and Frankenstein is pleased but anxious: 'Alas! to me the idea of an immediate union with my Elizabeth was one of horror and dismay' (p.157). Autumn brings a reunion with Henry, but 'how great was the contrast between [them]!' (p.159). Henry is alive to the beauty of the world – he loves nature 'with an eye of feeling and delight' (p.159), and is gifted with imagination. Frankenstein is morose and distressed at preparing another creation.

Q What does Frankenstein value about Elizabeth and Henry?

Chapter II

The beauty of spring temporarily affords Victor respite, but he returns to that key metaphor of nature in ruin: 'I am a blasted tree; the bolt has entered my soul' (p.165). As the friends travel to England, where Henry is going to study, Frankenstein is pursued by his conscience. We might question his refusal to take blame: 'I was guiltless, but I had indeed drawn down a horrible curse upon my head, as mortal as that of crime' (p.167). He exiles himself to the Orkneys and lives in a lowly hut, as the Creature did, trying to finish his work and fulfil his promise. However, this time he is making the ghastly creation in conscious knowledge of the outcome, and considers the task evil and joyless: 'now I went to it in cold blood, and my heart often sickened at the work of my hands' (p.169).

Q Examine Frankenstein's metaphor of the 'blasted tree' (p.165 – see also p.42). What does it reveal about how he feels about nature and himself?

Chapter III

Frankenstein finally reflects on the implications of his actions three years after the fact. While making the new mate, he considers the responsibility of being father, creator and god. In an horrifically violent act foreshadowing another key death, he rips apart and destroys the female as the Creature looks on in fury and despair. He demands Frankenstein keep his promise: 'You are my creator but I am your master' (p.172). He then vows to be with Victor on his wedding night.

Although Frankenstein feels some remorse, he dumps the torn-up female at sea, and drifts in his boat, wishing for death. He believes with lugubrious pleasure that his wedding night will be 'the fulfilment of my destiny. In that hour I should die, and at once satisfy and extinguish his malice' (p.173). His reverie is disrupted when he lands and is arrested for murder.

Q List the reasons Frankenstein gives for destroying his second creation. What else is destroyed by this act?

Chapter IV

In Ireland Frankenstein identifies Henry's corpse, knowing that he has been killed by the Creature; he then succumbs to a nervous breakdown for two months. Like an administering angel, Frankenstein's father arrives to help him and take him home. The paternal intervention cures the son's madness and despair, but the father has a perceptive glimpse of what Victor has initiated: 'You travelled to seek happiness, but a fatality seems to pursue you' (p.185).

Q 'Alas! Why did they preserve so miserable and detested a life?' (p.186). How does Frankenstein's 'return from death' compare with the Creature's experiences?

Chapter V

Frankenstein continues to experience guilt for his 'unhallowed acts' (p.189) while convalescing in Paris, and feels he has no right to human society. In counterpoint to his torment are Elizabeth's affectionate letters, but Victor is terrified to respond to his fiancée since the Creature's threat. He has hopes of marriage as a paradise but alludes to the apple from Eden being already eaten; yet he vows to tell his wife all his secrets after their wedding day. Worn by experience and the weight of forbidden knowledge, the couple are like another Adam and Eve after the fall. While their wedding is uneventful, Victor has presentiments of evil as night falls.

Q How is Frankenstein's emotional turmoil misread by others?

Chapter VI

That night the Creature murders Elizabeth, just as Frankenstein had destroyed the promised mate. Victor's father dies in grief and shock. Victor curses himself and attempts to tell his story to a magistrate.

Key point

In this crisis point, Victor at last finds himself in the Creature's position. Outcast, alone and misunderstood, he is feared as mad and dangerous. He becomes obsessed with vengeance, yet has no one to understand his story or share his pain.

Q 'Man, ... how ignorant art thou in thy pride of wisdom' (p.204). Who is 'ignorant' in his 'pride'?

Chapter VII

Frankenstein had previously desecrated graveyards, but personal experience has taught him now to respect the dead and contemplate whether human existence transcends physical limitations. His oath to live and kill his creation pleases the Creature, and they set off across the world in a cosmic chase of mutual torment, that can be thought of as a kind of *psychomachia* (epic allegorical battle of virtues and vices occurring within one's soul). Pursuit to the death becomes Frankenstein's purpose, and this life-denying act is reflected in the hostile icy landscape that is their final duelling ground. However, Frankenstein's health and strength are fading, which brings us back to his rescue by Walton, and his dying charge that his benefactor take over his vengeance and kill the Creature.

Q Why is the Creature so eager to be pursued? What is driving Frankenstein now?

Letter V

After a week, Frankenstein's narration stops and Walton resumes his address to Margaret. Victor's ensuing conversations are now recorded as letters, though he reads over and edits what Walton has been writing down. He also condemns Walton's curiosity to know precisely how the Creature was made (p.213). Frankenstein is consumed with desire for revenge against the Creature, and reflects on his dangerous ambitions (recalling Faust and Satan) and the sin of pride. Walton is eager to 'reconcile him to life' (p.214) in the hopes of retaining his newly found friend, but is refused: all our narrators are destined to be lonely souls.

Q What is the effect of the sudden, jarring return to Walton's narrative?

Letter VI

A series of crises begins for Walton as the hostile landscape closes in and the ship becomes icebound. Walton is terrified and fears for his life. He feels the responsibility of caring for his crew and laments that he has caused their danger (p.215). He is also tortured by the thought that his sister will not know his fate and the narrative we hold will never be read. Although Frankenstein endeavours to cheer and support him, and rally the despairing crew, Walton fears a mutiny.

Q 'He ... talks as if life were a possession which he valued' (p.216). How and to what extent do you think Frankenstein has valued life thus far?

Letter VII

As ice and danger close in, Walton's crew demand he turn back. Frankenstein makes an 'heroic' speech that averts mutiny temporarily, citing their glorious and noble undertaking and their captain's courage and fortitude. Walton asserts that he 'had rather die than return shamefully – my purpose unfulfilled' (p.218).

Key point

Walton's resolve mirrors Frankenstein's early ambitions and his closing passion to have revenge or to die trying.

Q How does Frankenstein's rousing speech to Walton's crew reflect on his own actions and motivation?

Letter VIII

Walton reluctantly consents to return, lamenting '[t]hus are my hopes blasted' (p.218).

Q Walton calls his enforced promise an 'injustice' (p.218). How are we to view this claim?

Letter IX

Key chapter

This significant final letter marks the death of Frankenstein. Walton mourns: 'I have lost my hopes of utility and glory; – I have lost my friend' (p.218). Victor's dying speech is a lengthy self-justification: his original act was a 'fit of enthusiastic madness' (p.219). He did the right thing by breaking his promise for the sake of mankind, and the Creature deserves to die so it may 'render no other wretched' (p.220). We may be more critical than Walton regarding the veracity of these claims. Frankenstein dies refusing to accept blame and still demanding Walton take over his revenge.

Walton finally meets Frankenstein's creation when the Creature appears literally as an interruption in the narrative (p.221), but finds him grieving and eloquent, not bent on destruction and murder. This arouses 'curiosity and compassion' in Walton, though he says repentance is useless. The Creature agrees and explains that he 'abhorred himself' (p.222). When Walton accuses him of lamenting only because he cannot continue to torment his creator, the Creature replies 'it is not thus' (p.223).

The rest of the narrative belongs solely to the Creature, who asks: 'Am I to be thought the only criminal, when all human kind sinned against me?' (p.224), but has nonetheless determined to commit suicide. He leaves across a sea of ice to a death by fire; his death will be a return to the elements from which he was created and his ashes will be blown away by the wind. As an 'unnatural' being made of a composite of misshapen and ill-matched parts, his self-sacrifice will be a moment of unity in nature. This is self-punishment but also a respite from sufferings – both selfish and martyr-like. Ultimately, his suicide fulfils Frankenstein's failed quest for vengeance, and releases Walton from the dying man's last request.

Q Compare the final self-justifying speeches of both Frankenstein and the Creature. What does each of them argue, and how convinced are you?

CHARACTERS & RELATIONSHIPS

Robert Walton

Key quotes

'I shall satiate my ardent curiosity with a part of the world never before visited.' (p.16)

'[H]ow gladly I would sacrifice my fortune, my existence, my very hope, to the furtherance of my enterprise.' (p.29)

At 28, Walton is a young, ambitious, adventure-hungry man. Thwarted in his desires to be a poet, Walton has pursued his childhood dream of a seafaring life and set out to explore the North Pole. In telling the full story to his sister of his own experiences, he also records the narrative of Frankenstein.

Walton's enthusiastic and aspiring nature reminds us of Frankenstein's own early ambitions and desires. Both have a Faustian willingness to give anything to achieve their ends; both anticipate bringing benefits to mankind, thus accruing respect and thanks as well as fame and fortune.

Walton offers a romanticised and sentimental view of Victor, who appears out of nowhere as the answer to Walton's wish for a friend. In some key respects, however, Walton differs from Frankenstein. He is aware of his social and personal responsibilities in caring for his crew and, importantly, gives up his dream to ensure their wellbeing. He does not lose touch with his family in pursuing his goal, and promises for Margaret's sake to be careful and stay safe.

Victor Frankenstein

Key quotes

'[T]he world was to me a secret which I desired to divine.' (p.38)

'Of what materials was I made, that I could thus resist so many shocks, which, like the turning of the wheel, continually renewed the torture?' (p.181)

'He seems to feel his own worth, and the greatness of his fall.' (p.214)

There is irony in the fact that Victor's name suggests success and triumph when we compare his desire for knowledge and fame with the tragedies his actions cause. He has links to Prometheus, Faust, and Milton's Satan and Adam; he is the precursor for other 'mad scientists' in literature, such as Robert Louis Stevenson's Dr Jekyll and H. G. Wells'

Dr Moreau. Like these characters, Frankenstein begins with good intentions, namely to banish human disease and stave off death. Selfish dreams of fame and glory, and dangerous desires – to play God and defy Nature in creating life and immortality – take over his mind.

Victor is only a young man not long out of university: he offers his tale to Walton (and us) as a warning against the dangers of the pursuit of knowledge. He gets lost in magical, 'unnatural' sciences and creates a being who comes to destroy everything and everyone he loves. His cautions still inform modern ethical concerns about the advance of science, from cloning and stem cell research to artificial intelligence and nuclear weapons. Frankenstein reminds us to consider all the possible consequences of our actions when we are playing with fire.

The Creature

Key quotes

'Who was I? What was I? Whence did I come? What was my destination?' (p.131)

'Was I, then, a monster, a blot upon the earth, from which all men fled and whom all men disowned?' (p.123)

'Life, although it may only be an accumulation of anguish, is dear to me, and I will defend it.' (p.102)

It is significant that only Frankenstein, the child William and the Creature use the word 'monster'. As a being without a name, the Creature becomes the repository for all the fears and anxieties of those he meets. They base their presumptions about him purely on his hideous appearance. Moreover, simply by existing, he transgresses natural boundaries. The expression 'back from the dead' evokes our fears about zombies, vampires and ghosts – the dark things that haunt our dreams and keep us awake at night. Quite literally for both his creators (Frankenstein and Mary Shelley) he was the stuff of nightmares.

However, his lack of a name also denotes his status as the outsider, the loner, the one who stands a head above the rest of the crowd. He desires only to understand himself and establish his identity and origins. He is therefore also the lost child searching for his real parents, the wrongly accused saviour punished for his kindnesses, and the refugee looking for somewhere to begin a new life and start a family.

The Creature makes us think about how we relate to our world and those around us and reconsider the ways we judge people on external qualities. He also makes us wonder why we pursue self-knowledge and how we construct our identities within our families, our social circles and the world at large.

Victor and the Creature

Key quotes

'You are my creator but I am your master.' (p.172)

'A new species would bless me as its creator and source; many happy and excellent natures would owe their being to me.' (p.55)

'I too can create desolation; my enemy is not invulnerable.' (p.144)

The relationship between the scientist and his Creature has become so close since 1818 that they have come to share the same name. This connection makes us reconsider some of the binaries we might otherwise use to divide them. Think about the two characters as creator/creature, artist/masterpiece, scientist/lab rat, parent/child, father/son, hero/villain, mentor/pupil and master/slave. Think, too, about the title of the novel in this regard – is *Frankenstein: The Modern Prometheus* a description of one or both characters, and does the colon between divide or unite the two names?

The lines of these binaries become blurred, and the member of the pair in power and control keeps changing. Frankenstein initially controls life and death over the other, but once the Creature comes into the world, he slowly exerts control over his creator. Yet for all his violence, he cannot compel Frankenstein to give him the one thing he craves: a mate. Their final chase across the globe underscores not just their interdependence, but their inability eventually to exist without the other. The two characters follow similar trajectories. Frankenstein is a slave to his work and later his promise; is prone to moral ambiguity; and becomes a new kind of scientist in defiance of his father and teachers; while his creation becomes educated, self-aware and desires a family of his own. Both characters spend the text pondering their own moral worth and the limits of knowledge of the world and of themselves. In considering their complex relationship, we will talk later about the idea of the *doppelgänger* and the shadow self: how something that seems to be your opposite and outside of you is really the core of what makes you what you are.

The Frankenstein family

Victor and his parents

Key quote

'Much as they were attached to each other, they seemed to draw inexhaustible stores of affection from a very mine of love to bestow upon me.' (p.35)

Victor's mother's family were called Beaufort ('beautiful-strong' in French) and Caroline 'possessed a mind of an uncommon mould' (p.34), caring for her dying father until his best friend Alphonse arrived to take her into his care. The child-woman becomes his wife, and is protected and worshipped as 'a fair exotic is sheltered by the gardener, from every rougher wind' (p.35).

This tender but closeting care is extended to their son, who is 'guided by a silken cord' (p.35), and then to adopted daughters Elizabeth and (to a lesser extent) Justine when Caroline is moved 'to act in her turn the guardian angel to the afflicted' (p.36). Caroline's early demise first sparks Victor's passion for conquering death. His mother and Elizabeth are grotesquely confused in Victor's nightmare (p.59) on the night that finally brings life to his creation. The Creature's murder of Elizabeth brings on the death of Victor's father, who had always been a stabilising force in his son's life; it adds fuel to Frankenstein's vengeful pursuit of his creation.

Victor and William

Key quotes

'William is dead! – that sweet child, whose smiles delighted and warmed my heart, who was so gentle, yet so gay! Victor, he is murdered!' (p.73)

'[M]onster! ugly wretch! you wish to eat me and tear me to pieces – You are an ogre – Let me go, or I will tell my papa.' (p.144)

William, the youngest child, is the darling of the family. It is a strange coincidence that the Creature should happen upon his creator's baby brother when he comes searching for Victor. The boy reveals his family name, and the Creature takes his first revenge.

The tragic death of William is ostensibly a death of innocence. However, the 'beautiful child' (p.144) is valued by his family for his looks, and it is this look of innocence that attracts the Creature's attention (he hopes the child is too young to be prejudiced against his own looks). But William has already been socially indoctrinated into making presumptions based on appearances, and partly it is his pride in himself and his family that reveals his origins and seals his fate.

Elizabeth Lavenza

Key quotes

'None could behold her without looking on her as of a distinct species, a being heaven-sent, and bearing a celestial stamp in all her features.' (p.36)

'All praises bestowed on her I received as made to a possession of my own ... my more than sister, since till death she was to be mine only.' (p.37)

Like Caroline, and later Justine Moritz, Elizabeth is adopted into the Frankenstein family as a child, which is framed as a benevolent 'rescue'. She is a 'garden rose among dark-leaved brambles' (p.36), a golden child from a noble family. Her rare beauty and angelic features endear her to all who encounter her: she is 'the living spirit of love' (p.40).

However, because her virtues are bound up in her beauty, Elizabeth becomes indicative of how we judge people by appearance. Indeed, she is objectified by most characters, and her self-effacing attitude – 'she forgot even her own regret in her endeavours to make us forget' (p.45) – renders her passive and subdued. From the first, she is a duty, a gift and a possession for Frankenstein. She is also labelled a healing tonic, a sedative to calm passion, and a balm to soothe people – not as a person in her own right.

Elizabeth's death is the culmination of the Creature's revenge killings; however, the description of her body not only objectifies her broken beauty, but recalls her murderer. The 'lifeless and inanimate' form and 'pale and distorted features' (p.199) are unsettlingly similar to descriptions of the Creature, and she dies on her 'bridal bier' as he does on his funeral pyre. In a sense, the Creature achieves what his creator refused him – he makes himself a mate in his own image and, in death, Frankenstein and he share a bride. (The 1994 movie *Mary Shelley's Frankenstein* took this symbolism and made it literal: Frankenstein reanimates his dead wife – spliced with Justine's body, no less – and the Creature momentarily believes him to have fulfilled his promise.)

Victor and Elizabeth

Key quote

> '[When Caroline] presented Elizabeth to me as her promised gift, I, with childish seriousness, interpreted her words literally and looked upon Elizabeth as mine – mine to protect, love, and cherish.' (p.37)

The words Victor uses to describe Elizabeth are curiously obsessive and confining. His love has a pride of ownership in it, and he views her as a part of himself and bound to him (not a whole, free, equal partner). Also, there is an incestuous nuance to their relationship whereby she is his 'more than sister' (p.37). Like his child-mother marrying her guardian father-figure, family relationships for the Frankensteins tend to become convoluted and unsettling. Victor does therefore wed his adopted sister, but she is killed by the Creature before the marriage can be consummated.

Henry Clerval

Key quotes

> '[A]lthough I loved him with a mixture of affection and reverence that knew no bounds, yet I could never persuade myself to confide to him …' (p.69)
>
> 'Excellent friend! how sincerely did you love me and endeavour to elevate my mind until it was on a level with your own!' (p.71)

In school Victor was immersed in scientific studies, but Henry was reading of knights and adventures and chivalry. Like his fictional heroes, Henry comes to embody noble and humanitarian virtues – he is 'so perfectly humane, so thoughtful in his generosity' (p.40). In fact, in later life he arrives just in time to 'rescue' Victor when the latter is first traumatised by the 'success' of his experiment, and then again after the fateful promise to the Creature.

However, because Frankenstein never fully confides in his friend, he loses the benefit of Henry's moral grounding. Henry can only try to be understanding and sympathetic. Part of the tragedy of Henry's death is that Frankenstein never gave him the opportunity to save his friend from his dangerous course of action.

Justine

Key quotes

'She is very clever and gentle, and extremely pretty … her mien and her expressions continually remind me of my dear aunt.' (p.67)

'Alas! who is safe, if she be convicted of crime?' (p.81)

Justine takes over the mothering role in caring for William, but it is her devotion to the child that first sparks suspicions of her involvement in his death. Framed by the Creature in a fit of rage, for all she represented that he could not have, the beautiful, placid girl stands trial with dignity and is executed for a crime she did not commit.

Justine is a socially liminal (between two states) character: although nominally of the Frankenstein family, she is not of their social standing. She was adopted, as a kindness on Caroline's part, from a lower-class family where she was under-appreciated (like Elizabeth). However, she is still a paid servant and works for her keep. Like William, she is sacrificed to atone for the sins of Frankenstein against nature and of mankind against the Creature, but she is sustained in her darkest hour by a faith in God and in her own innocence that neither of her murderers possesses.

The De Lacey family

Key quote

'They loved and sympathised with one another; and their joys, depending on each other, were not interrupted by the casualties that took place around them.' (p.134)

Felix gave himself up after helping a Turkish merchant in Paris escape an unjust death sentence, but the De Lacey family was exiled from France forever. Living impoverished in a small cottage in Germany, the family still love and care for each other. However, when the Creature begs the blind father for asylum and friendship, Felix mistakes the approach for an attack, and beats the Creature while Agatha faints and Safie runs away. The family flee the cottage soon after, and we hear no more of them.

The history of the cottagers resonates with other key events in the novel. In this family, too, there is the motif of the benevolent but ineffective father, the absent mother, the introduction of an adopted sister who is to become a daughter-in-law, and a son who, with the best of intentions, leads to the downfall of the whole family. Safie's experiences learning a new language and trying to comprehend foreign social and cultural behaviours coincide with the Creature's own education and development. She is also initially an outsider like the Creature, but her beauty allows her to be accepted and welcomed into a new country and family, while his hideous appearance only ostracises him further.

The Creature and the cottagers

Key quote

'If such lovely creatures were miserable, it was less strange that I, an imperfect and solitary being, should be wretched.' (p.113)

It is through observing the lives of the cottagers that the Creature learns of human interaction, domesticity and relationships. This discovery of family structures and home life is coupled with a growing understanding of human civilisation, including language, literature, music, philosophy and husbandry. It is also through their unconscious influence that he develops an awareness of human emotions such as love, loyalty, anger and grief, and of universal concepts such as instincts, ageing and death.

The De Lacey family members allow the Creature to connect himself with humanity, but he also realises, tragically and irrevocably, that he is unable to be part of it. They represent a life of social, romantic and familial cohesion that he will never know: they have what he will never possess. When they reject him, he retaliates by burning down their property as the symbol of their home and home life. A thwarted Promethean, he uses fire destructively against humans this time.

Krempe and Waldman

Key quotes

Krempe: 'He was an uncouth man, but deeply imbued in the secrets of his science.' (p.47)

Waldman: '… an aspect expressive of the greatest benevolence …' (p.48)

Krempe is a professor of natural philosophy at the university in Ingolstadt and, like Frankenstein's father, his contempt for his student's eccentric and outdated studies only provokes Victor to continue his research. The novel is concerned with our tendency to make presumptions based on appearance, and Frankenstein's instant dislike of Krempe because of his unpleasant looks highlights the younger man's limited outlook. Moreover, Krempe's later comparison of himself to Frankenstein (as modest when young and conceited when knowledgeable; p.70) suggests teacher and pupil have more in common than the latter might like to admit.

Unlike Krempe, Waldman is handsome and charming. As a teacher he is inspiring and supportive; Victor finds him a 'true friend' and exults in his instruction and attention. However, it is Waldman's speech in praise of new science that forms 'the words of the fate – enounced to destroy me' (p.49). In this, Waldman unwittingly takes on the role of Mephistopheles the tempter to Frankenstein's Faust, enticing the young scholar towards a dark, dangerous path.

THEMES, IDEAS & VALUES

As a novel of ideas, *Frankenstein* explores the ambiguously attractive nature of knowledge. Life is full of 'big' questions and no answers. While uncertainty about the meaning of life may stimulate us to find out more, it can also provoke deep anxiety about the limits of what can be known. Humans devise culturally shared ways to manage 'big' questions: religious beliefs, agreed values about right and wrong supported by laws, philosophical speculation, political structures and education systems.

People continually attempt to develop reasonable ways to share questions about origins and purpose. How can we be involved in exploring life's possibilities? How can we understand why some lives blossom while others are crushed by life's challenges? Why do some people deliberately choose to destroy life rather than protect it? What about questions of cloning or genetic manipulation, unimaginable to Frankenstein? Do you think he would be interested?

Nature

Key quote

> '[M]any things will appear possible in these wild and mysterious regions, which would provoke the laughter of those unacquainted with the ever-varied powers of nature ...' (Victor, p.31)

The novel explores a dilemma: can we be content with domestic life ticking along according to Nature's 'immutable laws' with 'little alteration' as Elizabeth describes it (p.66) – or do we want to know nature's secrets, like Walton and Frankenstein, even if they seem unattainable or dangerous?

Key point

For the Romantic writers of this period, the natural world is of paramount importance in sustaining human life and enhancing understanding. Nature and humans share an organic relationship: when we enter into the presence of awe-inspiring natural sights, fundamental questions come to mind, such as: Where (and what) is a Creator? Is there a value and purpose to life? How do humans fit in to the scheme of things ... and whose scheme is it?

Nature and nurture

Key quotes

'[M]y senses were gratified and refreshed by a thousand scents of delight, and a thousand sights of beauty.' (Creature, p.119)

'[H]ow much happier that man is who believes his native town to be the world, than he who aspires to become greater than his nature will allow.' (Victor, p.54)

The notion of a person's 'nature' (inherent qualities) driving actions is often presented in antithesis to the idea that we are shaped and motivated by the social and physical environment in which each of us lives and is nurtured. The model in which human 'nature' dominates is found in myth, fairytale and popular romance, where an apparently lowly person turns out to have intrinsic virtues and heroic qualities. 'Nature' will be recognised and rewarded (an overlooked young squire pulls the sword from the stone and becomes King Arthur). Conversely, an inherently warped nature may cloak itself in virtue but one day be exposed and punished. 'Nurture' may be required to bring out inherent good qualities and eradicate or suppress undesirable ones – neglect may do the reverse.

Frankenstein admits reluctantly that aspiration may exceed a person's natural capacity (p.54). Driven by enthusiasm and technical know-how, but unregulated by natural feelings, he commits an unnatural act in creating life from death. The Creature appears physically unnatural but has his own innocent nature. Frankenstein's failure to fulfil his obligations and nurture his creation, together with the consequent hostile impact of the outside world upon the Creature, eventually outweighs the Creature's inherently good qualities.

Natural man

Key quotes

'I felt light, and hunger, and thirst, and darkness.' (Creature, p.106)

'The mildness of my nature had fled, and all within me was turned to gall and bitterness.' (Creature, p.142)

The Creature epitomises Rousseau's 'Natural man' in his coming to consciousness (Volume Two, Chapters III, IV and V are based directly on Rousseau's ideas). The Creature is naturally curious and benevolent until he's injured by repeated rejection. He reads Milton and identifies first with Adam, the perfect human who is thrown out of paradise, and then (appalled at his own repulsive looks and ill-treatment) with Satan, the Archfiend. Frankenstein dooms his unnatural man/thing to a solitary reviled life. Note the key passage for the idea of 'natural man' when the Creature moves from a state of 'utter and stupid despair' to hatred of all humans (pp.140–3).

Geography of the psyche

Key quotes

'Happy, happy earth! fit habitation for gods ...' (Creature, p.118)

'It was a most beautiful season ... but my eyes were insensible to the charms of nature.' (Frankenstein, p.56)

The dichotomy of nature versus nurture is complicated by the relationships we have with our environments. Sometimes the natural world seems to reflect us or our feelings (we feel good and it's a sunny day); sometimes it affects or even infects us (we feel sad and it's cold and raining, or is it *because* it's cold and raining?). Romantic writers constantly balanced inner feelings and states with outer natural conditions in a subtly dramatic interplay.

Key point

Romantics also contributed to a refashioning of the ancient concept of 'Mother Nature' by combining a benevolent goddess-parent sense of the natural world with a more abstract elemental 'force' (like a god but not specifically associated with Christian, or any other, religion). This force engages human senses and emotions in a powerful way: Nature is both uplifting to the individual spirit (nurturing and relaxing) and overwhelmingly terrifying in its unpitying vastness (arousing thrilling tension).

While natural sights (especially mountains, lakes and waterfalls) promote feelings of peace, calmness, innocent joy and goodwill, humans simultaneously perceive that they are dwarfed by the landscape and that a peaceful scene may easily become dangerous in a storm, flood, fire or avalanche. Nature is imbued with the spirit of the *Sublime* – that unknowable force, 'a power mighty as Omnipotence' (p.97).

Note how seasonal and diurnal (day/night) cycles become metaphors for characters' emotional states and impulses:

- Spring renews the Creature's hopes of establishing life with the cottagers, and signals Frankenstein's temporary revival of spirits twice in the story.
- Frankenstein's frenzied unnatural creativity occurs in summer (although he doesn't notice).
- In autumn the female Creature is destroyed and Frankenstein's own marriage is blasted as the season turns to winter.
- Twice the Creature is rejected in winter.

There are situational metaphors, where an environment becomes the 'scene' for highly charged emotional encounters:

- Frankenstein confronts the Creature in mountains, on glaciers, on ice sea.
- Storms are precursors to Frankenstein's encounters with the Creature.
- Fog and mist give Walton only a dim glimpse of the Creature, preparing for the final encounter when he still cannot bear to look directly at such 'unearthly' ugliness (p.221).
- Sun brings joy for the Creature (p.142).
- Wind is described as a fierce uncontrollable force, symbolic of the rush of excited emotions, as an 'avalanche' (Creature, p.140), a 'hurricane' (Frankenstein, p.55).
- The hostile, cold sea is a metaphor for the sea of life. Walton speaks of Frankenstein in terms of a sea voyage, now 'in wreck' (p.28).
- The blasted tree is used as a metaphor for Victor's ruined nature (p.42; p.165).

Love

Shelley provides many examples of how humans respond to kindness and affection, either made manifest or denied and thwarted. Sexuality was more problematic to write about in the 19th century than now. Romantic poets were not the first to discover the power of love, although Percy Shelley's essay 'On Love' (1815) is one of the fullest expressions of ideas about the subject. It is centrally relevant to *Frankenstein*. For Percy Shelley, love is:

> the powerful attraction towards all that we conceive, or fear, or hope beyond ourselves … the bond and sanction which connects not only man with man, but with everything that exists. We are born into the world, and there is something within us, from the instant that we live, that more and more thirsts after its likeness. Hence in solitude, or in that deserted state when we are surrounded by human beings, and yet they sympathise not with us, we love the flowers, the grass, and the waters and the sky … by their inconceivable relation to something within the soul, [they] awaken the spirits to a dance of breathless rapture, and bring tears to the eyes … (edited from text in *Portable Romantic Reader*, pp.105–7)

This idea of love is illustrated in the Creature's specific desire for a partner: 'if any being felt emotions of benevolence towards me, I should return them an hundred and an hundredfold. For that one creature's sake I would make peace with the whole kind!' (p.148).

Parents and children

Key quotes

'I was their plaything and their idol …' (Frankenstein, p.35)

'No father had watched my infant days, no mother had blessed me with smiles and caresses …' (Creature, p.124)

Victor and his Creature grow up in starkly different circumstances, illustrating two models of development, through nature and nurture (see notes above). Victor enjoys a caring family environment, which epitomises 'nurture' as a key shaper of a child's development. The rejected 'baby/adult' Creature is forced to live wild and parentless. The cottage family life, as the Creature observes it, is united and loving. Significantly, Safie, the foreigner, is welcomed as a new daughter.

Companionship and sexuality

Key quotes

'I felt sensations of a peculiar and overpowering nature: they were a mixture of pain and pleasure, such as I had never before experienced ...' (Creature's first sensation of sexual desire as part of romantic love, p.111)

'[H]er gentleness, and soft looks of compassion, made her a more fit companion for one blasted and miserable as I was.' (Victor and Elizabeth before marriage, p.194)

Shelley could not have written frankly about sex and be widely published, despite leading a life of relative sexual freedom herself. She is able to represent passionate feelings, nonetheless, in dramatic description. The Creature's capacity to imagine and desire passion is in marked contrast to Victor's polite emotional coolness towards Elizabeth. She mentions his reluctance to marry in her letter (pp.191–2); Victor and Elizabeth are worn down by a sadness that estranges them. When they finally marry, Elizabeth experiences anxiety about the honeymoon (p.197). The Creature, on the other hand, is most explicit about wanting a mate. It will link him as a human being 'to the chain of existence and events' (p.150).

Friendship

Key quotes

'I greatly need a friend who would have sense enough not to despise me as romantic, and affection enough for me to endeavour to regulate my mind.' (Walton, p.20)

'[W]e are unfashioned creatures, but half made up, if one wiser, better, dearer than ourselves – such a friend ought to be – do not lend his aid to perfectionate our weak and faulty natures.' (Frankenstein to Walton, p.30)

'I had feelings of affection, and they were requited by detestation and scorn.' (Creature, p.172)

Both Walton and Frankenstein value friendship highly – Walton even calls its absence a 'most severe evil' (p.19). They both consider a close male friend (provided he is their equal in age, class and education) to be paramount to their own sense of self as an adult and their emotional and intellectual balance. Were Walton not so lonely, he might have been less eager to idolise Frankenstein, giving a more critical commentary to the story he hears. Part of Frankenstein's downfall is also this want of the steadying and stimulating effect of a close friendship. After neglecting his family to obsess over his study and experiments, he grows away from his friend Henry, who might have checked his wild schemes and passions.

Knowledge

Key quotes

'Of what a strange nature is knowledge. It clings to the mind, when it has once seized on it, like lichen on the rock.' (Creature, p.123)

'I shall satiate my ardent curiosity.' (Walton, p.16)

Curiosity is an irrepressible driving force. Someone wise once said that facts are not information, information is not knowledge, and knowledge is not wisdom. The novel explores this theme in several ways, depending on the way knowledge arrives, what drives the seeker (curiosity, ambition, pride), and what is the outcome of discovery. Frankenstein seeks after the 'forbidden' knowledge of the secrets of life heedless of the possible consequences. Yet near his death he does not seem to have learnt anything: he warns Walton not to pursue knowledge *at all* (p.54), as though knowledge itself were to blame for his ordeal. For his part, Walton fails to glean any self-knowledge about the limits of aspiration from Frankenstein's story: instead, he feels he returns 'ignorant and disappointed' (p.218). The Creature's intellectual development is a fast accumulation of useful information, transformed through rejection into tormenting knowledge of his isolation from humanity.

Aspiration

Key quotes

'Do I not deserve to accomplish some great purpose?' (Walton, p.17)

'It was the secrets of heaven and earth that I desired to learn ...' (Frankenstein, p.39)

For Shelley's Promethean seekers, aspiration is the ambition to acquire knowledge pushed further by pride. Walton and Victor think they can achieve anything because they are dedicated to purposes that mark them out as special. Both anticipate universal praise. In contrast, the Creature merely dreams about being accepted by humanity. It is only after he is rejected that he aspires to destruction.

Key point

Characters like Frankenstein, who aspire beyond normal human capacity and suffer for their daring, may be depicted as either the Overreacher (who is punished by God) or the Wanderer (doomed never to find rest).

The Overreacher

Key quotes

'[Y]ou cannot contest the inestimable benefit which I shall confer on mankind ...' (Walton, p.16)

'I trod heaven in my thoughts, now exulting in my powers, now burning with the idea of their effects.' (Victor to Walton, p.214)

Walton's boastful assumption is matched by Frankenstein's aspiration to play God and 'pour a torrent of light into our dark world' (p.55). For both men, obsessive desire outweighs caution. It also brings up the question of what humans *can* know – is there a limit? Is it just because we are naturally limited in our capacity to understand, or because some supreme being has set limits on our knowing? These thoughts form the basis of the tragic debate in Milton's *Paradise Lost,* and continue to tease contemporary minds. The archangel Lucifer's pride leads him to challenge God and lose both Heaven and his bright name. Adam and Eve disobey God and lose paradise and innocence but gain human knowledge. It's a perennial problem for humanity – knowledge brings the possibility of both benefits and troubles.

Tellingly, Frankenstein compares himself with Lucifer in pride, Satan in his fall (p.214). Shelley and her readers would also make an immediate connection with Dr Faustus, the classic type of overreacher in the Western literary tradition (see 'Background & Context').

The Wanderer

Key quotes

'I shall kill no albatross, therefore do not be alarmed for my safety, or if I should come back to you as worn and woeful as the "Ancient Mariner".' (Walton, p.21)

'And now my wanderings began, which are to cease but with life.' (Frankenstein, p.205)

Although Walton experiences arctic isolation temporarily, Victor and his Creature epitomise the doomed, restless figure of the Wanderer, epitomised in early Christian tradition as Ahazuerus, or the Wandering Jew (a man who mocked Christ on his way to Crucifixion and then repented, accepting the role of eternal witnessing storyteller). Key Romantic figures of the Wanderer are the captain and crew of the legendary *Flying Dutchman* and Coleridge's Ancient Mariner, all of whom are denied rest for their supposed sins.

Beauty and ugliness

Key quotes

'[A]ll the kindness which [Justine's] beauty might otherwise have excited was obliterated in the minds of the spectators by the imagination of the enormity she was supposed to have committed.' (Victor, p.83)

'Why did you form a monster so hideous that even *you* turned from me in disgust?' (Creature, p.133)

Outer appearance may prejudice perceptions of inner worth. Even today, people are psychologically disposed to equate outer beauty in a person (highly subjective *and* culture-bound as it is) with positive character attributes. The correlation has persisted over centuries in the formula 'fair within and fair without', with predictably negative social consequences for anyone not meeting supposed physical norms. The Romantic aesthetic of the Sublime was anything but an exception to the rule, and Shelley clearly criticises this impulse throughout *Frankenstein*.

One can track the Creature's developing sense of his own monstrous appearance: he terrifies himself (p.116); he tries to be rational about hideousness (p.135); he hopes that communication through language will compensate for physical ugliness (p.116); he confronts his creator for making his form ugly (p.133). The true monstrosity lies in Frankenstein's terrible parody of creation, the cruelty he has committed underlined for the reader by the Creature's sensitivity to his 'filthy' form. When he points out that 'God, in pity, made man beautiful and alluring, after his own image' and that even Satan had companions 'to admire and encourage him' (p.133), his words attract the reader's sympathy. Any act of kindness in the crucial period of the Creature's development might have steered him from his violent path, but he faces only revulsion from those he meets. Prejudged as evil (because he is ugly), the Creature decides to become evil.

It is difficult to accept that Victor could ever have imagined that his enormous Creature, made from bits of different dead bodies, would be anything but ugly. His suddenly turning away from the Creature in disgust at the moment of success (Volume One, Chapter V) seems one of the weaker moments of the novel, but it underscores Victor's blindness to anything but his own ego – at least until the moment that his obsession takes on a life of its own. The Creature's 'ugliness' goes deeper than his appearance. His unnatural status as a *living* thing made of *dead* things is terrifying. He is neither one nor the other, yet he is *both* at once, another *liminal* character; he is *uncanny,* recognisable as human but (in a way we can't define) not human. (Freud wrote an essay on *The Uncanny,* essential reading for Gothic literature.)

Responsibility and guilt

Key quotes

'Man, you shall repent of the injuries you inflict.' (Creature to Victor, p.173)

'You accuse me of murder, and yet you would, with a satisfied conscience, destroy your own creature.' (Creature, p.103)

'*I was guiltless,* but I had indeed drawn down a horrible curse upon my head, as mortal as that of crime.' (Victor, p.167, emphasis added)

'Responsibility' is experienced by everyone in both positive and negative ways. It is associated with standing by an agreement you've made to do something or carrying out a task that falls to you in life – everything from occasionally feeding the neighbours' pets through to looking after other people and shouldering adult roles at work and in the community. In a negative sense, 'responsibility' is what you have to accept if you are guilty of doing something wrong or causing injury, either intentionally or by accident. It may lead to punishment. Admitting responsibility may also involve feeling remorse and repentance for wrongdoing. It requires maturity and moral perception to accept and admit guilt.

In her Epigraph, Shelley pinpoints a creator's responsibility towards a creature that did not ask to come into existence (quoting Adam's words to God in *Paradise Lost*: *Book X* – p.1). Victor struggles with the reality of his guilt for irresponsible experimentation but seems perplexed by the Creature's murders – are they his fault directly? Note the double-take when he hears that Justine has confessed to William's murder (p.87). He goes unpunished by society because he keeps silent about the Creature until after the murder of Elizabeth. By this time it is too late and he is not believed.

Note the key passage in which Frankenstein glimpses the Creature during a storm and 'realises' it must be William's killer (pp.78–9). Notice the way he transfers guilt immediately to his Creature but can't exonerate himself completely: he calls the Creature his 'own vampire', his 'own spirit let loose from the grave', 'forced' to kill.

Other characters are not so ambiguous about responsibility. For example:

- Elizabeth accepts responsibility for looking after Frankenstein's family when Victor's mother dies, and later for indirectly causing William's death.
- Clerval takes on the responsibility of nursing Victor back to health.
- Walton reluctantly puts responsibility for the crew's safety above his own ambition.

Free will versus destiny

Key quotes

'There is something at work in my soul, which I do not understand.' (Walton, p.22)

'You may give up your purpose, but mine is assigned to me by Heaven.' (Victor, p.219)

Frankenstein circles around the fundamental enigma of life that intrigues its protagonist: Who or what drives the engine? What is the soul? Can Victor create a soul or spirit for the Creature? The work of atheistic Romantic writers is saturated with emotionally charged spiritual and supernatural imagery, underpinning the idea of the Sublime we've already identified. Victor claims that 'nothing can alter [his] destiny' (p.31). He cites 'Chance – or rather the evil influence, the Angel of Destruction' (p.47) as the cause of his ruin, lying in wait to catch him the moment he leaves the protection of home. He sees himself as the site of a universal moral battle between what he terms the 'spirit of good' and his doomed destiny: neither of which are himself, his fault, or under his control.

Victor fluctuates throughout the text between self-accusations and a desire to lay the blame elsewhere – upon fate, 'evil spirits' or the Creature. In his deathbed speech, he claims he does not find his past conduct 'blameable' (p.219). The Creature also blames 'an impulse, which I detested, yet could not disobey' (p.222), but he calls his motivation 'selfishness' and 'willingly chosen'. The difference lies in the Creature's willingness to claim responsibility for choices made, compared to Frankenstein's ultimate rejection of any blame for his actions. To the end, they are driven by this view of life – Frankenstein's spirits of 'vengeance' fail him (p.219) and he dies unfulfilled and unwillingly, whereas the Creature owns his guilt and inflicts his own punishment in killing himself, thus completing his creator's quest.

Matters of life and death

Key quotes

'To examine the causes of life, we must first have recourse to death.' (Victor, p.52)

'Life and death appeared to me ideal bounds, which I should first break through.' (Victor, p.55)

'I devote myself, either in my life or death, to his destruction.' (Victor, p.204)

Further questions of responsibility are raised by characteristically Gothic issues about taboo and transgression, irresolvable guilt, and an obsessive focus on death. You'll notice a more elegiac Romantic tone in Victor's speculations about Clerval's death (p.161). Consider these two key passages:

- Victor plans and builds his Creature (pp.52–9) – this is pure Gothic horror designed to make the reader feel revulsion, as much as for Victor's unimaginative callousness as for gory details.
- Clerval's sensitivity to different aspects of the natural sublime, followed by Victor's meditation on Clerval (pp.160–1).

Frankenstein creates life for the wrong reasons, through pride and without responsibility. Hence it is appropriate that his new life is formed out of dead things, which (significantly) hold no 'supernatural horrors' (p.52) for him. He suppresses his creative imagination (what the Romantics knew as 'fancy') to focus all his attention on the deadly research. Ordinarily, respect for the dead is a natural human impulse, reinforced by strong taboos against desecration. When he finally enters a graveyard for the 'right' reasons, to weep for his dead family and friends, his distorted emotions are expressed in the form of a vow to pursue his Creature to the death and avenge their murders (p.205).

DIFFERENT INTERPRETATIONS

Different interpretations arise from different responses to a text. Over time, a text will give rise to a wide range of responses from its readers, who may come from various social or cultural groups and live in very different places and historical periods. These responses can be published in newspapers, journals and books by critics and reviewers, or they can be expressed in discussions among readers in the media, classrooms, book groups and so on. While there is no single correct reading or interpretation of a text, it is important to understand that an interpretation is more than an 'opinion' – it is the justification of a point of view on the text. To present an interpretation of the text based on your point of view you must use a logical argument and support it with relevant evidence from the text.

Critical viewpoints

Key quote

'The writer of it is, we understand, a female; this is an aggravation of that which is the prevailing fault of the novel; but if our authoress can forget the gentleness of her sex, it is no reason why we should; and we shall therefore dismiss the novel without further comment.' (*The British Critic* 1818, p.438)

Since *Frankenstein* was first published, critical interest has been piqued by the idea of a teenage girl writing such a powerful and influential novel that is driven by male narrators. Mary Shelley originally published anonymously. When her identity was revealed, several early reviewers were eager to blame faults in the text on the author's gender: the suggestion was that the style and content of the novel were too violent, uncouth and subversive for a female to have penned.

Interestingly, these were the sorts of critiques her famous mother Mary Wollstonecraft encountered when she published her feminist treatise *A Vindication of the Rights of Woman* (1792), and she, too, first published her work anonymously, writing in response to powerful and influential male authors. As with her mother's writings, modern feminist scholars have celebrated Shelley's literary achievement and consequently engaged in close gendered readings of the text.

Leading on from this, scholarly biographical interest explored Shelley's relationship to her parents' ideas and to contemporary Romantic and revolutionary influences. Feminist-inflected discussions of Shelley as a political and social commentator have taken biographical ideas in other directions, exploring Shelley the writer as defined in varying degrees by her female status historically, as wife and mother (Homans 1986). Other key interpretations in this area are found in Sandra Gilbert and Susan Gubar (1979), William Veeder (1986) and Anne K. Mellor (1988), with a collection of thought-provoking essays edited by Harold Bloom (1985).

Another important line of enquiry has followed Promethean ideas of knowledge and power, with the dangerous stereotype of 'mad scientist' emerging, especially in 20th-century film versions. The novel's ideas about creating artificial life informed a new 19th-century genre called science fiction. The theme of Frankenstein's relationship with his horrific creation has also been tied to wider issues of monstrosity (Baldick 1987) as well as to questions of responsibility, social ostracism and violence, and to concern for the 'heroic pathos' typified by the Creature (Bloom 1971).

Developments in contemporary science are a rich field for ideas relating back to Shelley's original, as is the continuing debate about society's dangerous, fear-inducing undercurrents (Grixti 1989). Finally, it is useful to review how Shelley's story has been refashioned to reflect contemporary interests and anxieties, as we now do when studying the work (O'Flinn, in Botting 1995).

You will find pathways to explore a range of critical approaches on the websites indicated (see 'References & Reading') and essay collections like Behrendt's (1990). Below are two interpretations you could explore further.

Two interpretations

Reading 1: Mother love and creativity

Key quote

'Where were my friends and relations? No father had watched my infant days, no mother had blessed me with smiles and caresses ...' (Creature p.124)

Mary Shelley famously called this novel her 'hideous progeny' (*Author's Introduction* 1831, p.10) – as an author, she was thinking about her art in terms of a parent dealing with a terrible and terrifying child. Frankenstein also describes his story as 'the remains of my hideous narration' (p.201), and calls himself the 'author of unalterable evils' (p.95) with regard to his creation of life. The act of creating, writing and making art is being connected here with both parenting and childbirth; the roles of artists and creators are likened to those of mothers and fathers, with texts and artworks as their 'children'.

In her teens, Shelley suffered two traumatic childbirths and deaths of babies, and her own mother died giving birth to her. The horrors of birth and the terrors of ensuing parenthood shape the central act of creation in her novel. One of the reasons why the Creature's genesis disturbs us is because it upsets our normal expectations about birth and reproduction. Not only is it the father-figure bestowing life on a 'hideous progeny', but this offspring is both an infant and an adult, a collection of parts yet a strange new whole; finally, he is born dead – yet alive. This contradictory and perverse representation of parent and child stays with us as we consider other families in the novel, and the ties of love and loyalty that unite other fathers and mothers and sons and daughters influence the way we regard Frankenstein and his Creature.

The novel abounds with dead and/or absent mothers, weak benevolent fathers, devoted brothers and sisters, and adopted children. In contrast, the Creature has no parents to care for him and no family to protect and support him. 'Born' as a fully grown adult, he is conscious of his entire infancy and is able to remember all that we forget as babies, from his first feelings and observations, to his initial ideas and growing sense of self: 'I felt light, and hunger, and thirst, and darkness; innumerable sounds rang in my ears' (p.106). He is fundamentally self-taught, and his 'childhood' can be seen as a metaphor for the entire advent and advance of human civilisation, including the ability to communicate. Acquiring the power of language and the written and spoken word culminates in the Creature being able to tell his own story.

Written in a literary competition with Percy Shelley and Lord Byron, *Frankenstein* was literally a response to the Romantic male writer. The protagonist's passions, ambitions and sensibilities recall the creative, bohemian, unconventional lifestyles of these writers and other contemporary poets, as does his unsettling misogynistic sense of ownership over Elizabeth, and the emphasis on male bonding: 'I desire the company of a man who could sympathise with me; whose eyes would reply to mine' (p.19).

In drawing parallels between Shelley's own life and the few female characters in this novel (they are given relatively little space and speech and often die young), it is interesting to note that it is the exotic, marginalised foreigner Safie who most reminds us of our author, rather than the demure Elizabeth or the helpless Justine. Mary Shelley fled her home for love, against the wishes of her father and in defiance of social conventions, and when we recall how Safie's experiences are likened to those of the Creature, we can consider some more complex possibilities about how gender is being constructed here.

Feminist scholars Sandra Gilbert and Susan Gubar toyed with the idea that the 'male monster may really be a female in disguise' (Gilbert and Gubar 1979, p.237). Considering the biblical allusions and Miltonic references in *Frankenstein*, they realised how the Creature can be aligned with Eve: his desire to know unleashes sin, and he is judged by physical appearance more harshly than other men might be.

In a novel exploring the complex relationship of a creator to their creation, Shelley's explanation of her novel as her hideous progeny has also led critics to locate the author in Frankenstein himself. Ellen Moers reads the novel as 'a woman's mythmaking on the subject of birth' (Moers 1979, p.81). In this interpretation, the possibility of seeing birth as an unnatural and horrible act (rather than a sentimental romanticised one) is raised. Shelley is reimagining her own traumatic experiences of miscarriage and childbirth as a horror story – a gothic, violent, self-destructive warning.

Victor's acting as 'mother' is seen as a speculation on how men might deal with the process of bringing a child into the world (along with the anxieties and pressures of mothering). It may also be a reiteration that mothering is a role that should rightly belong to women.

In light of this, it is worth considering that, despite the male narrators, Shelley imagined a female readership for her novel. Although she is silent, Walton's sister is ultimately the recipient of the narrative. Moreover, Shelley wrote the 1831 Introduction in which she publicly reclaimed her progeny for herself under her own name. This seems fitting for a novel that is so intimately concerned with questions of responsibility, ownership and the power of creation.

Reading 2: The divided self

Key quote

> 'I considered the being whom I had cast among mankind and endowed with the will and power to effect purposes of horror ... nearly in the light of *my own vampire*, my own spirit let loose from the grave and *forced* to destroy all that was dear to me.' (Frankenstein, p.78, emphasis added)

One interesting way to read *Frankenstein* is from the psychological perspective of a divided self. Frankenstein opens his narrative to Walton by stating the central theme of divided beings that recognise they are somehow united – how can they be reintegrated, made 'whole' and finished? His purpose, he says, is 'to seek one who fled from me'.

Gothic horror makes provision for such an idea in the stock character of the *doppelgänger* (a word imported from folklore into German Romanic art – literally, your double who goes with you). It is traditionally thought of as a spectral warning of death to the person who is haunted by it: Poe used it brilliantly in his story *William Wilson*. English Romantics like Blake and Shelley knew this association but chose to do something more complex with it – a century before the subject was tackled by psychoanalysis, notably Freud's theory of the Ego and Id, Rank's study of the Double and Carl Jung's ideas about the Shadow archetype.

Victor claims that the Creature fled from him, yet we remember that it was Victor who first fled in horror from his creation as soon as it came to life (p.58) and his dream turned to disappointment. What had he created? How could he have been blind to the monstrosity he was assembling? Of the three psychoanalytical models mentioned above, Jung's archetype of the Shadow enables us to explore these questions raised by the conflicted relationship between the two doomed beings.

An 'Archetype', in Jungian terms, is defined as a structuring pattern in the psyche, expressed most vividly in the cluster of attributes we recognise belonging to gods and other powerful characters in mythology, paintings, statues, even films and advertisements, etc. (for example, the god of war, the goddess of love, a wise father-figure, a healer). Individuals express archetypal 'hard-wiring' most obviously in instinctive behaviour during life's crisis moments: clustered around birth, death, separation, parenthood, etc. Jung argued that people can also become obsessively and emotionally overpowered by a particular situation or idea: this leads to 'inflation' as they imagine themselves to have the power of an Archetype. They think they are godlike and can do anything. When they fail (as they inevitably do during inflated thinking), they plunge from the heights to the depths of despair. Victor's is a classic pattern of inflation (being the adored child, the brilliant student ... the creative overreacher), then the breakdown (followed by the destructive obsession with revenge). In the Romantic period, archetypal imagery flooded into consciousness from the depths of the psyche through dreams and painting, in poetry and music. Jung was especially interested in this expression of proto-psychology. (If you are interested to find out more, research William Blake's unique mythology of archetypal figures.)

Walton observes that Frankenstein has 'a double existence' (p.30). He makes a sensible inference from what he sees of Frankenstein's changing expressions that the man is torn by some inner conflict. This is accurate in one respect: Frankenstein's mind is burdened and conflicted because of things he's done that stimulate both pride and regret in him. What Walton cannot yet know is that Frankenstein's double existence is literally the existence of a 'double' who looks nothing like him but is intrinsically part of the same person (as Hyde would later be for Dr Jekyll in Stevenson's popular Victorian version of the same theme).

The hostile but symbiotic (mutually needing) relationship between Victor and his Creature models Jung's formulation of the Shadow as a complementary but shunned part of Victor's whole personality. The more that is shunned and hidden, the darker the Shadow becomes. Victor's Ego consciousness (the man he shows to the world) is the brilliant young natural philosopher and Walton's heroic wanderer. The unnamed Creature expresses vital Shadow aspects of the whole Self called 'Victor Frankenstein'.

Why is the Shadow especially terrifying to the Ego? Because it contains all the negative aspects, faults and weaknesses that the Ego wants to bury. Frankenstein's Shadow 'Creature' grows in menace in proportion to Victor's rejection of what it represents about him. Specifically, he is naturally passionate, emotional, expressive, violent and sexual. He can commit murder and desire a mate.

The Creature's macabre game of tag with Frankenstein confirms their oneness, as Victor explains to Walton: 'sometimes he himself, who feared that if I lost all trace of him I should despair and die, left me some mark to guide me' (p.207). He also expresses deep reluctance to kill the Creature – it has to be couched in religious necessity: 'I pursued my path towards the destruction of the daemon *more as a task enjoined by heaven, as a mechanical impulse of some power of which I was unconscious*, than as the ardent desire of my soul' (p.208, emphasis added).

Reading *Frankenstein* from this perspective enhances its tragic conclusion for both Victor and the Creature. Victor dies too soon and in the wrong frame of mind to attempt reconciliation. The two halves can never be integrated – except, perhaps, in the mind of a compassionate reader of Shelley's text.

QUESTIONS & ANSWERS

This section focuses on your own analytical writing on the text, and gives you strategies for producing high-quality responses in your coursework and exam essays.

Essay writing – an overview

An essay is a formal and serious piece of writing that presents your point of view on the text, usually in response to a given essay topic. Your 'point of view' in an essay is your interpretation of the meaning of the text's language, structure, characters, situations and events, supported by detailed analysis of textual evidence.

Analyse – don't summarise

In your essays it is important to avoid simply summarising what happens in a text:

- A **summary** is a description or paraphrase (retelling in different words) of the characters and events. For example: 'Macbeth has a horrifying vision of a dagger dripping with blood before he goes to murder King Duncan'.
- An **analysis** is an explanation of the real meaning or significance that lies 'beneath' the text's words (and images, for a film). For example: 'Macbeth's vision of a bloody dagger shows how deeply uneasy he is about the violent act he is contemplating – as well as his sense that supernatural forces are impelling him to act'.

A limited amount of summary is sometimes necessary to let your reader know which part of the text you wish to discuss. However, always keep this to a minimum and follow it immediately with your analysis (explanation) of what this part of the text is really telling us.

Plan your essay

Carefully plan your essay so that you have a clear idea of what you are going to say. The plan ensures that your ideas flow logically, that your argument remains consistent and that you stay on the topic. An essay plan should be a list of **brief dot points** – no more than half a page. It includes:

- your central argument or main contention – a concise statement (usually in a single sentence) of your overall response to the topic. See 'Analysing a sample topic' for guidelines on how to formulate a main contention.
- three or four dot points for each paragraph indicating the main idea and evidence/examples from the text. Note that in your essay you will need to *expand* on these points and *analyse* the evidence.

Structure your essay

An essay is a complete, self-contained piece of writing. It has a clear beginning (the introduction), middle (several body paragraphs) and end (the last paragraph or conclusion). It must also have a central argument that runs throughout, linking each paragraph to form a coherent whole.

See examples of introductions and conclusions in the 'Analysing a sample topic' and 'Sample answer' sections.

The introduction establishes your overall response to the topic. It includes your main contention and outlines the main evidence you will refer to in the course of the essay. Write your introduction *after* you have done a plan and *before* you write the rest of the essay.

The body paragraphs argue your case – they present evidence from the text and explain how this evidence supports your argument. Each body paragraph needs:

- a strong **topic sentence** (usually the first sentence) that states the main point being made in the paragraph
- **evidence** from the text, including some brief quotations
- **analysis** of the textual evidence explaining its significance and **explanation** of how it supports your argument
- **links back to the topic** in one or more statements, usually towards the end of the paragraph.

Connect the body paragraphs so that your discussion flows smoothly. Use some linking words and phrases like 'similarly' and 'on the other hand', though don't start every paragraph like this. Another strategy is to use a significant word from the last sentence of one paragraph in the first sentence of the next.

Use key terms from the topic – or synonyms for them – throughout, so the relevance of your discussion to the topic is always clear.

The conclusion ties everything together and finishes the essay. It includes strong statements that emphasise your central argument and provide a clear response to the topic.

Avoid simply restating the points made earlier in the essay – this will end on a very flat note and imply that you have run out of ideas and vocabulary. The conclusion is meant to be a logical extension of what you have written, not just a repetition or summary of it. Writing an effective conclusion can be a challenge. Try using these tips:

- Start by linking back to the final sentence of the second-last paragraph – this helps your writing to 'flow', rather than just leaping back to your main contention straight away.
- Use synonyms and expressions with equivalent meanings to vary your vocabulary. This allows you to reinforce your line of argument without being repetitive.

- When planning your essay, think of one or two broad statements or observations about the text's wider meaning. These should be related to the topic and your overall argument. Keep them for the conclusion, since they will give you something 'new' to say but still follow logically from your discussion. The introduction will be focused on the topic, but the conclusion can present a wider view of the text.

Essay topics

1 In popular culture, the name 'Frankenstein' has often been wrongly attributed to the Creature instead of his creator. Examine the relationship between these two characters: how alike do they prove to be?

2 *Frankenstein* is full of ambitious characters; for example, the determined scientist, the brave explorer, and the Creature that 'wants to know'. What rewards for and dangers of pursuing ambitions appear in the novel?

3 'Frankenstein always had good intentions but does not consider the consequences of his actions.' Do you agree?

4 Mary Shelley chose to write her novel in epistolary form (as a series of letters). How do Walton's letters help us understand the story? What do they contain, and what do they reveal?

5 'Ultimately, Frankenstein is punished for having created an abomination against Nature.' Do you agree?

6 Frankenstein's Creature wants to understand what he is. What does he discover about himself and about the nature of being human?

7 Although written by a woman, *Frankenstein* is mostly concerned with male characters. What roles do women play in the novel? How do female experiences affect the story?

8 'Frankenstein's Creature was not inherently evil – society and his experiences gradually made him that way.' Do you agree?

9 "I would not that a mutilated one should go down to prosperity" (p.213). Frankenstein is speaking of his story, not the Creature. How is storytelling in the novel being related to his act of creation?

10 "I have myself been blasted in these hopes, yet another may succeed" (p.220). In your opinion, is *Frankenstein* more a cautionary tale or an inspirational one?

Analysing a sample topic

"Remember I am not recording the vision of a madman." Is Frankenstein the quintessential 'mad scientist'?

This topic is asking you to evaluate the character and motivations of Frankenstein, and to consider how scientific progress and the pursuit of knowledge are being presented in the text. Think through the key concepts of science and madness that your introductory sentences will consider:

- 'Quintessential' means 'in its most typical and concentrated form'. What defines a typical 'mad scientist' in popular culture (and in some remakes of this novel)?
- How does the Frankenstein we meet in the text compare to this stereotype?
- Despite his protestations, does he display any traits or take any action that might be considered 'mad'?

Preparatory notes for main discussion

Begin by exploring Frankenstein's early attitudes to science and learning. What motivates him to pursue his schemes? How does he view science? He is young, excited and has noble aspirations – do these facts counteract any claims that his original passion for knowledge is actually a form of 'madness'?

Focus on Chapter IV (where the topic quote is located) and then the key scene opening Chapter V when he first brings the monster to life. This section has informed many depictions of the 'mad scientist' creating in his laboratory. How does this scene actually compare to the stereotype? Look in detail at Frankenstein's descriptions of his emotions and the reasons he gives for doing what he does.

Examine Frankenstein's later behaviour, and the consequences of his 'vision' coming to life. How are these related to his status as a scientist, and his desire for knowledge? Does he descend into madness? Are there moments where he is driven mad? (He often claims so.)

Consider some of his key actions here: the promise to build a 'mate', the destruction of her, the final vengeful pursuit of the creature. Is Frankenstein still a scientist at these junctures? How 'mad' are his decisions? How do they compare to the experiences of other characters (for example, Felix ruining his family, the Creature killing Elizabeth, Walton trekking to the North Pole)?

Conclusion

Reflect on your original introductory answer to the topic – is Frankenstein a quintessential mad scientist? You have considered the stereotype and compared the character to it. You have also looked at how he approaches science and learning, and examined whether any of his characteristics or actions in the text might be called 'mad'. Draw these discoveries together now to form your conclusion. For example:

- you might have argued Frankenstein *is* the quintessential mad scientist because his character and actions informed all later versions and his actions are obsessive and unreasonable;
- or you might have claimed he does *not* fulfil the stereotype, although he commits certain acts of madness or falls into insanity at some point(s);
- or you might have denied the topic entirely and shown Victor to be driven not by madness at all but by a misguided passion for learning and an understandable love for his family and the human race.

Your conclusion will remind us how Frankenstein fits or breaks the mould of the 'mad scientist', and how complex the question of identifying madness is in this text.

SAMPLE ANSWER

'Ultimately, Frankenstein is punished for having created an abomination against Nature.' Do you agree?

In Mary Shelley's novel, Frankenstein insists on his deathbed that he does not find his past conduct 'blameable', and claims his Creature 'showed unparalleled malignity and selfishness, in evil'. His refusal to accept responsibility for having defied the natural order in bringing the dead back to life is also a refusal to accept the consequences as a punishment. However, the Creature says, 'I was benevolent and good; misery made me a fiend', and even holds himself accountable for the tragedies that occurred. Ultimately, Frankenstein cannot be punished because he refuses to accept responsibility for what he has done, and although he considers his creation to be evil and unnatural, the Creature believes it is only in appearance that he is an abomination.

Frankenstein spends much of the narrative evading blame and responsibility for his actions. He claims 'Destiny was too potent, and her immutable laws had decreed my utter and terrible destruction', but accusing fate allows him to avoid accepting guilt himself. He also holds his father and teachers responsible for not warning him about the dangers of learning, and excuses his original act of creation as 'a fit of enthusiastic madness'. However, many of the decisions that lead to the tragic deaths of his family and his demise are his own choice. Frankenstein nonetheless blames the Creature's malevolence and inherent evil qualities for the series of tragedies, despite the fact that he created the murderer. Ultimately, he cannot view the destruction of everything he loves as a punishment for his scientific transgressions because he never fully acknowledges his actions were wrong.

In contrast, the Creature realises that his motivations for revenge were selfish and 'willingly chosen', and recognises the horror of what he has done: 'I abhorred myself'. He owns his guilt, but asks, 'Am I to be thought the only criminal, when all human kind sinned against me?' Unlike Frankenstein, the Creature shows remorse at the end of the narrative and does believe he is being punished. However, he is not always being condemned for what he has done (as might have been the case with Frankenstein). Even before he commits any crimes, he is constantly punished for *what he is* – but this is unfair. You can make choices about your actions, but you cannot help what you are or what you look like. Thus the Creature sees other characters commit acts of violence and has even been a victim of crimes himself, but he is always condemned first because of his terrible appearance.

His own creator believes from the outset that he is evil and unnatural. Frankenstein designed the Creature to be beautiful, but when he comes to life, 'breathless horror and disgust' fill him. The Creature offends against the laws and beauty of nature in his ugliness and physical monstrousness. When William is murdered, Frankenstein presumes at once his creation is the killer because '[n]othing in human form could have destroyed that fair child', and this prejudice is mirrored in the way others react to the Creature; for example, the man who shoots him when he rescues a drowning girl, and Felix beating him when he begs the blind father for friendship.

However, the Creature believes his 'heart was fashioned to be susceptible of love and sympathy'. Left alone and friendless after his 'birth', the Creature teaches himself about human society and civilisation. He asks, 'Who was I? What was I?' and his fundamental questions about what it means to be human and initial endeavours to appreciate nature, learn about culture and seek love suggest it is only his hideous exterior that makes him appear an abomination. He is not inherently horrifying: it is only fear, misunderstanding and human prejudice that make him defy his gentle nature. Society's violent and unjust reactions to him and rejection of him meant that '[e]vil thenceforth became [his] good'.

While his physical appearance is terrifying, the novel *Frankenstein* suggests there are other things in the world more abominable and unnatural than the Creature, such as prejudice, injustice and self-deception. Frankenstein (like other characters in the novel) is prejudiced against things that are not beautiful, treats the Creature unfairly because of this, and deceives himself into thinking this is justified behaviour. Although Frankenstein will not admit guilt and therefore accept punishment even when dying, his original reckless actions destroy everything he loves. Therefore any retribution he earns is ultimately brought down upon others, including the Creature's imminent self-inflicted death. The Creature may be physically abominable, but he proves to have a more noble nature than his self-deceiving creator.

REFERENCES & READING

Text

Shelley, Mary (1818, 1831) 2003, *Frankenstein*, ed. Maurice Hindle, Penguin Classics, London.

Intertexts

Blake, William (1790) facsimile 1975, *The Marriage of Heaven and Hell*, Oxford University Press, London.

Godwin, William (1805) 1975, *Caleb Williams*, New English Library, London.

——(1793), *Enquiry Concerning Political Justice*.

Goethe, Johann Wolfgang von (1787) 1962, *The Sorrows of Young Werther*, Signet, New York.

——(1790+) 1911, *Faust*, Parts I and 2, Ward Lock, London.

Milton, John (1674) 1975, *Paradise Lost*, Norton Critical Edition, New York.

Rousseau, Jean-Jacques (1781) 1953, *Confessions*, transl. J. M. Cohen, Penguin, Harmondsworth.

Wollstonecraft, Mary (1792) 1975, *Vindication of the Rights of Woman*, ed. Miriam Kramnick, Penguin, Harmondsworth.

Further reading

Baldick, Chris 1987, *In Frankenstein's Shadow: Myth, Monstrosity and Nineteenth-Century Writing, Oxford,* Clarendon Press.

Behrendt, Stephen C. (ed.) 1990, *Approaches to Teaching Shelley's Frankenstein* (Approaches to Teaching World Literature series), The Modern Language Association of America, New York.

An excellent companion text to this Insight Text Guide. Essays, focused specifically on teaching strategies, extend discussion of ideas and suggest further areas for exploration.

Bloom, Harold 1971, *The Ringers in the Tower*, University of Chicago Press, Chicago and London (Chapter 8).

——(ed.) 1985, *Modern Critical Views. Mary Shelley*, Chelsea House, New York.

Botting, Fred (ed.) 1995, *New Casebooks. Frankenstein*, Macmillan, London.

Useful collection, both new and extracted from key critical texts.

Davenport-Hines, Richard 1998, *Gothic. Four Hundred Years of Excess, Horror, Evil and Ruin*, Fourth Estate, London.

Florescu, Radu 1975, *In Search of Frankenstein*, New English Library. London.

Excellent but dated overview of Mary Shelley's life, writing of novel; lists plays and films on theme; illustrations, bibliography, ideas for further discussion.

Gilbert, Sandra M. and Gubar, Susan 1979, *The Madwoman in the Attic*, Yale University Press, New Haven.

Grixti, Joseph 1989, *Terrors of Uncertainty. The Cultural Contexts of Horror Fiction*, Routledge, London.

Haining, Peter 1979, *The Man who was Frankenstein*, Muller, London.

Hugo, Howard E. (ed.) 1957, *The Portable Romantic Reader*, Penguin (Viking Portable Library), Harmondsworth.

King, Stephen 1982, *Danse Macabre*, London, Futura.

Mellor, Anne 1988, *Mary Shelley: Her Life, Her Fiction, Her Monsters*, Routledge, New York.

Moers, Ellen 1979, 'Female Gothic' in Levine and Knoepflmacher (eds), *The Endurance of Frankenstein, Essays on Mary Shelley's Novel*, Berkeley, University of California Press.

Mulvey-Roberts, Marie (ed.) 1998, *The Handbook to Gothic Literature*, Macmillan, London.

Punter, David 1996, *The Literature of Terror: The Gothic Tradition* (2nd edition, Vol. I), London, Longman.

Stoker, John 1980, *The Illustrated Frankenstein*, Reed, Sydney.

Tomalin, Claire 1980, *Shelley and his World*, Thames and Hudson, London.

Uglow, Jenny 2002, *The Lunar Men. The Friends who made the Future 1730–1810*, Faber and Faber, London.

Veeder, William 1986, *Mary Shelley & Frankenstein: The Fate of Androgyny*, University of Chicago Press, Chicago.

Wischhusen, Stephen (ed.) 1975, *The Hour of One. Six Gothic Melodramas*, Gordon Fraser, London.

Contains a script for one of the popular stage adaptations of Frankenstein in 1820s, with the Monster leaping into an erupting volcano (Mt Etna) on stage at the end. Contains illustration of classically costumed actor Mr O. Smith as 'The Monster'.

Films

Read Florescu, for filmography, and Chapter 9, *The Frankenstein Films*, for interesting visual images and overview of early film versions to 1974.

Read MLAA essay (Winston Dixon), *The Films of 'Frankenstein'*, which has a clear description of 1910 Edison film shots (thought lost).

Frankenstein 1931, dir. James Whale, Universal Studios. The classic version; Creature played by Boris Karloff. Find *James Whale's Frankenstein, The Film Classics Library*, Macmillan, London, 1974, for a shot-by-shot reconstruction of the film with full dialogue.

Gothic 1986, dir. Ken Russell, Vestron Pictures. Brilliant, disturbingly weird, surreal recreation of life with the Shelleys and Byron at Villa Diodati, and Mary Shelley's 1816 nightmare recreated.

Websites

www.crossref-it.info/textguide/Frankenstein/7/402 – An excellent comprehensive study site with many links to background material. Good critical analysis and recent critical approaches.

www.FrankensteinFilms.com/ – The Frankenstein movie and Monster horror film site. Interesting material on all films, including Branagh's (1994), Andy Warhol's (1974) and Dean Koontz's (2004), plus surveys of recent films on the theme like *Godsend* (2004), *The 6th Day* (2000) and *The Island* (2005).